I0670147

CCE-FL

Comptroller of the Currency
Administrator of National Banks

Fair Lending

Comptroller's Handbook

January 2010

CCE

Fair Lending

Appendixes

Introduction

Examiners use these procedures to evaluate a national bank's compliance with the Fair Housing Act (FH Act), Equal Credit Opportunity Act (ECOA), and the Federal Reserve Board's Regulation B. This booklet contains the Federal Financial Institutions Examination Council's (FFIEC) "Interagency Fair Lending Examination Procedures," and appropriate OCC supplemental material.

General Guidelines

These procedures are intended to provide a flexible framework to be used in fair lending examinations conducted by the FFIEC agencies. They are also intended to guide examiner judgment, not to supplant it. The procedures may be augmented by each agency as necessary to ensure effective implementation. For example, the OCC uses statistical modeling and regression analysis in selected examinations to assist in determining whether race, national origin, or sex was a factor in credit decisions.

The OCC uses a risk-based approach to identify national banks and mortgage subsidiaries[1] for comprehensive fair lending examinations. During each supervisory cycle, examiners perform a fair lending risk assessment in each national bank. Based on the risk assessment, examiners may initiate full scope fair lending examinations or other appropriate supervisory activities to ensure compliance with fair lending laws and regulations.

To complement the supervisory office (SO) risk assessment process, the OCC also selects banks and mortgage subsidiaries for comprehensive fair lending examinations using a risk-based and random sample screening process that supplements the on-going supervisory office efforts. First, the OCC uses the Home Mortgage Disclosure Act (HMDA) data to select banks according to criteria related to the risk of fair lending violations. The examination scoping procedures typically are not applicable to such risk-based examinations since the screening process identifies a loan product(s) and a prohibited basis for review.

Second, the OCC randomly selects a sample of banks and mortgage subsidiaries to receive comprehensive fair lending examinations. For

---

[1] Throughout this booklet, bank or banks will include subsidiaries.

examinations of randomly selected banks, examiners use the examination scoping procedures in this booklet. If the supervisory office or OCC policy has designated certain banks, products, market areas, etc., as priorities to examine, OCC examiners make scoping decisions accordingly. Absent such guidance, OCC examiners who use the scoping procedures should treat them as a menu from which sections should be selected, not as a recipe to be followed entirely in every examination.

Specific to the OCC, this booklet:

- Directs examiners to take different approaches depending on whether a bank is selected based on risk, via the screening process, or randomly.
- Contains threshold procedures for determining whether the OCC should use statistical modeling for the comparative analysis.
- Contains procedures and supporting materials for determining whether banks are in compliance with:

  - **Requirements in Regulation B (12 CFR 202) Regarding Other Illegal Limitations on Access to Credit.** A number of provisions in Regulation B are intended to facilitate access to credit by providing consumers with certain rights (for example, the right to open a credit account in a birth given name) or by imposing on banks certain obligations (for example, not to alter terms of a credit account adversely because the account holder retires). Noncompliance can harm consumers. Some of Regulation B's consumer rights are not stated explicitly in terms of a prohibited basis (for example, discounting or excluding "protected income," in violation of 12 CFR 202.6(b)(5)). The OCC additionally evaluates the possible role of a prohibited basis in such violations. (In this booklet, only violations involving a prohibited basis are referred to as "discrimination.") There is a checklist in appendix K of this booklet for reviewing compliance with these provisions of Regulation B and guidance in the examination procedures for using the checklist.

  - **Technical Requirements in Regulation B (12 CFR 202).** Regulation B requires banks to use certain practices that do not directly relate to evaluating the applicant's creditworthiness (for example, retaining records of credit transactions). These requirements are important, in part, because they facilitate creation of records that support comparative file review and help consumers obtain their rights. Examiners evaluate compliance with these provisions when setting the overall supervisory strategy for the bank. There is a checklist in appendix L of this booklet to assist in these reviews and guidance in the examination procedures for using the checklist.

The procedures emphasize racial and national origin discrimination in residential transactions, but the key principles are applicable to other prohibited bases and to nonresidential transactions. These procedures focus on analyzing bank compliance with the broad, anti-discriminatory requirements of the ECOA and the FH Act.

If there are pending administrative proceedings or government enforcement litigation involving the bank's fair lending compliance, generally a fair lending examination should not begin.

The OCC may conclude that a referral to the U.S. Department of Justice (DOJ), a referral to the U.S. Department of Housing and Urban Development (HUD), or an OCC enforcement action is appropriate to address possible illegal disparate treatment or some other fair lending violation, even if the OCC fails to follow any of this booklet's procedures or practices. Neither is such a failure sufficient by itself to rebut information suggesting that a violation occurred. The OCC will base its conclusions on the reliability and totality of the information and circumstances.

Overview of Fair Lending Laws and Regulations

The ECOA prohibits discrimination in any aspect of a credit transaction. It applies to any extension of credit, including those to small businesses, corporations, partnerships, and trusts.

The ECOA prohibits discrimination based on:

- Race or color.
- Religion.
- National origin.
- Sex.
- Marital status.
- Age (provided the applicant has the capacity to contract). Although ECOA prohibits discrimination on the basis of age in the extension of credit, it permits banks to favor "elderly" applicants. Regulation B defines "elderly" as 62 years old or older.
- The applicant's receipt of income derived from any public assistance

program.

- The applicant's exercise, in good faith, of any right under the Consumer Credit Protection Act.

The Federal Reserve Board's Regulation B, found at 12 CFR 202, implements the ECOA. Regulation B describes lending acts and practices that are specifically prohibited, permitted, or required. Official staff interpretations of the regulation are found in supplement I to 12 CFR 202.

The FH Act prohibits discrimination in all aspects of "residential real-estate related transactions," including but not limited to:

- Making loans to buy, build, repair, or improve a dwelling.
- Purchasing real estate loans.
- Selling, brokering, or appraising residential real estate.
- Selling or renting a dwelling.

The FH Act prohibits discrimination based on:

- Race or color.
- National origin.
- Religion.
- Sex.
- Familial status (defined as children under the age of 18 living with a parent or legal custodian, pregnant women, and people securing custody of children under 18).
- Handicap.

HUD's regulations implementing the FH Act are found at 24 CFR 100. Because both the FH Act and the ECOA apply to mortgage lending, banks may not discriminate in mortgage lending based on any of the prohibited factors in either list.

Under the ECOA, it is unlawful for a bank to discriminate on a prohibited basis in any aspect of a credit transaction, and under both the ECOA and the FH Act, it is unlawful for a bank to discriminate on a prohibited basis in a residential real-estate-related transaction. Under one or both of these laws, a bank may not, because of a prohibited factor:

- Fail to provide information or services or provide different information or services regarding any aspect of the lending process, including credit availability, application procedures, or lending standards;
- Discourage or selectively encourage applicants in inquiries about or applications for credit;
- Refuse to extend credit or use different standards in determining whether to extend credit;
- Vary the terms of credit offered, including the amount, interest rate, duration, or type of loan;
- Use different standards to evaluate collateral;
- Treat a borrower differently in servicing a loan or invoking default remedies; or
- Use different standards for pooling or packaging a loan in the secondary market.

A bank may not express, orally or in writing, a preference based on prohibited factors or indicate that it will treat applicants differently on a prohibited basis. A violation may still exist even if a bank treated applicants equally.

A bank may not discriminate on a prohibited basis because of the characteristics of:

- An applicant, prospective applicant, or borrower;
- A person associated with an applicant, prospective applicant, or borrower (for example, a co-applicant, spouse, business partner, or live-in aide); or
- The present or prospective occupants of either the property to be financed or the characteristics of the neighborhood or other area where property to be financed is located.

The FH Act requires banks to make reasonable accommodations for a person with disabilities when such accommodations are necessary to afford the person an equal opportunity to apply for credit.

Additionally, when the OCC becomes aware of violations of state fair lending laws, the OCC will take appropriate supervisory or enforcement action.

Types of Lending Discrimination

The courts have recognized three methods of proof of lending discrimination under the ECOA and the FH Act:

- Overt evidence of disparate treatment,
- Comparative evidence of disparate treatment, and
- Evidence of disparate impact.

Disparate Treatment

The existence of illegal disparate treatment may be established either by statements revealing that a bank explicitly considered prohibited factors (overt evidence) or by differences in treatment that are not fully explained by legitimate nondiscriminatory factors (comparative evidence).

Overt Evidence of Disparate Treatment. There is overt evidence of discrimination when a bank openly discriminates on a prohibited basis:

> Example: A bank offered a credit card with a limit of up to $750 for applicants aged 21 through 30 and $1,500 for applicants over 30. This policy violated the ECOA's prohibition on discrimination based on age.

There is overt evidence of discrimination even when a bank expresses — but does not act on — a discriminatory preference:

> Example: A lending officer told a customer, "We do not like to make home mortgages to Native Americans, but the law says we cannot discriminate and we have to comply with the law." This statement violated the FH Act's prohibition on statements expressing a discriminatory preference as well as Section 202.4(b) of Regulation B, which prohibits discouraging applicants on a prohibited basis.

However, otherwise-prohibited overt language and distinctions are permissible in "Special-Purpose Credit Programs." For more information, refer to appendix C, section B.

<u>Comparative Evidence of Disparate Treatment</u>. Disparate treatment occurs when a bank treats a credit applicant differently based on one of the prohibited bases. It does not require any showing that the treatment was motivated by prejudice or a conscious intention to discriminate against a person beyond the difference in treatment itself.

Disparate treatment may more likely occur in the treatment of applicants who are neither clearly well qualified nor clearly unqualified. Discrimination may more readily affect applicants in this middle group for two reasons. First, if the applications are "close cases," there is more room and need for bank discretion. Second, whether or not an applicant qualifies may depend on the level of assistance the bank provides the applicant in completing an application. The bank may, for example, propose solutions to credit or other problems regarding an application, identify compensating factors, and provide encouragement to the applicant. Banks are under no obligation to provide such assistance, but to the extent that they do, the assistance must be provided in a nondiscriminatory way.

> Example: A control group couple applied for an automobile loan. The bank found adverse information in the couple's credit report. The bank discussed the credit report with them and determined that the adverse information, a judgment against the couple, was incorrect because the judgment had been vacated. The control group couple was granted their loan. A prohibited basis group couple applied for a similar loan with the same bank. Upon discovering adverse information in the prohibited basis group couple's credit report, the bank denied the loan application on the basis of the adverse information without allowing the couple to discuss the report.

The foregoing is an example of disparate treatment of similarly situated applicants, apparently based on a prohibited factor, in the amount of assistance and information the bank provided.

If a bank apparently has treated similar applicants differently on the basis of a prohibited factor, it must provide an explanation for the difference in treatment. If the bank's explanation is found to be not credible, the agency may find that the bank intentionally discriminated.

Illegal disparate treatment exists when applicants are "similarly situated," but are treated differently on a prohibited basis. Typically, a disfavored applicant who is "similarly situated" is as well or better qualified than a favored one, though factors other than qualifications may be relevant. In fair lending examinations, examiners usually focus on whether the deficiency the bank cited to justify the unfavorable treatment of an applicant from a prohibited basis group also existed for any favorably treated control group applicant who was no better qualified. If not, such an inconsistency is termed "apparent disparate treatment," indicating that the situation may be discrimination or it may have an innocent explanation. "Apparent" is not a synonym for "obvious" or "blatant."

If the bank shows that, at the time of the credit decisions, it considered a legitimate difference between the applicants that justified treating one more favorably than the other, examiners conclude that the applicants were not actually "similarly situated," so no illegal disparate treatment occurred. There are numerous lawful reasons why an applicant from one race, gender, etc., might be treated less favorably than one from another group. The anti-discrimination laws do not require uniform treatment of all customers.

Redlining is a form of illegal disparate treatment in which a bank provides unequal access to credit, or unequal terms of credit, because of the race, color, national origin, or other prohibited characteristic(s) of the residents of the area in which the credit seeker resides or will reside or in which the residential property to be mortgaged is located. Redlining may violate both the FH Act and the ECOA.

Disparate Impact

When a bank applies a racially or otherwise neutral policy or practice equally to all credit applicants, but the policy or practice disproportionately excludes or burdens certain persons on a prohibited basis, the policy or practice is described as having a "disparate impact."[2]

> Example: A bank's policy is not to extend loans for single family residences for less than $60,000.00. This policy has been in effect for 10 years. This minimum loan amount policy is shown to disproportionately exclude potential applicants based on race from consideration because of their income levels or the value of the houses in the areas in which they live.

---

[2] Disparate impact has been referred to more commonly by the OCC as "disproportionate adverse impact." It is also referred to as the "effects test."

The fact that a policy or practice creates a disparity on a prohibited basis is not by itself proof of a violation. When the OCC finds that a bank's policy or practice has a disparate impact, the OCC seeks to determine whether the policy or practice is justified by "business necessity." The justification must be manifest and may not be hypothetical or speculative. Factors that may be relevant to the justification could include cost and profitability. Even if a policy or practice that has a disparate impact on a prohibited basis can be justified by business necessity, it still may be found to be in violation if an alternative policy or practice could serve the same purpose with less discriminatory effect. Finally, evidence of discriminatory intent is not necessary to establish that a bank's adoption or implementation of a policy or practice that has a disparate impact is in violation of the FH Act or ECOA.

These procedures do not call for examiners to plan examinations to identify or focus on potential disparate impact issues. The guidance in this introduction is intended to help examiners recognize fair lending issues that may have a potential disparate impact. Guidance in appendix G, "Other Types of Discrimination Analyses," provides details on how to obtain relevant information regarding such situations, and methods to evaluate and follow up, as appropriate.

Referral to the DOJ or HUD

ECOA requires the OCC to refer matters to the DOJ "whenever the OCC has reason to believe that one or more creditors has engaged in a pattern or practice of discouraging or denying applications for credit in violation of section 1691(a)" of ECOA, which states ECOA's basic prohibitions against discrimination. Additionally, ECOA requires the OCC to notify HUD whenever there is reason to believe that both ECOA and the FH Act have been violated and the suspected violations have not been referred to DOJ. Furthermore, Executive Order No. 12892 requires that HUD be notified "upon receipt of information . . . suggesting a violation" of the FH Act, and that such information also be forwarded to DOJ if it "indicate[s] a possible pattern or practice of discrimination in violation of the act. . ." The Concluding the Examination section of this booklet provides guidance to examiners and supervisory offices on how to respond to a bank's apparent violation of a fair lending law.

Examination Procedures for Setting the Examination Scope

Background

Establishing the proper scope for a fair lending examination is critical.

In setting the examination scope, examiners consider the loan product(s), market(s), decision center(s), time frame, and prohibited basis and control group(s) to be analyzed during the examination. These procedures refer to each potential combination of those elements as a "focal point." Examiners first identify all of the focal points that could be reviewed during an examination. Then, from among those, examiners select the focal point(s) to be examined based on risk factors, priorities established in these procedures or by OCC policy, the record from past examinations, and other relevant guidance. Examiners also consider the bank's compliance management system as it relates to fair lending.

Existing information may be used to expedite setting the scope. Also, scoping may disclose the existence of circumstances, such as a bank's use of credit scoring or a large amount of residential mortgage lending, when a different examination approach may be more efficient than the procedures set forth in this booklet. Statistical modeling, regression analysis, or other statistical techniques that the OCC has developed may be used in such circumstances.

When selecting focal points for review, examiners may determine that the bank has performed "self-tests" or "self-evaluations" related to specific lending products. The difference between "self-tests" and "self-evaluations" is discussed in appendix H, "Using Self-Tests and Self-Evaluations to Streamline the Examination." Banks must share all information regarding "self-evaluations." Regulation B at 12 CFR 202.15 and the FH Act at 24 CFR 100.140 cover self-tests and indicate that the report or results of a "self-test" is privileged and if such materials are shared with the OCC, the privilege would be waived. However, Section 607 of the Financial Services Regulatory Relief Act of 2006 (12 USC 1828(x)) allows banks to share such privileged information with its federal regulatory agency during supervisory activities without waiving, destroying, or otherwise affecting that privilege for other third parties, such as private litigants.[3] Therefore examiners may request all relevant information related to "self-evaluations," and a bank may provide the report or results of a "self-test" that the bank has performed to examiners without waiving any privilege that attaches to such materials, except for the agency. Information from "self-evaluations" or "self-tests" may allow the examination to be streamlined. Refer to the aforementioned "Using Self-Tests and Self-Evaluations to Streamline the Examination" for additional details.

In determining the scope of an examination, examiners consider:

- The OCC's priorities and the supervisory office's long-term strategy for evaluating whether the bank's lending activities comply with the fair lending laws.
- The products, markets, and decision centers that are important to the bank.
- Availability of information that supports reliable results.
- Useful information that adds significantly to the cumulative picture of whether the bank complies with fair lending laws.
- Whether lending activities have undergone significant changes in personnel, operations, or underwriting standards.

The fair lending laws broadly prohibit discrimination on all the bases listed in the Introduction. The OCC enforces these laws to the fullest extent. However, the OCC places particular emphasis on evaluating whether there is discrimination against racial or national origin groups in residential lending. Scoping, for those examinations when the scope has not been selected in the screening process described on pages 1 and 2, should always consider whether there is a reasonable likelihood of obtaining a useful, reliable result by examining for racial or national origin discrimination in:

- Residential underwriting or
- The rates, terms, or conditions of residential loans made.

However, analysis of a nonresidential product (or of a prohibited basis group other than race or national origin) is appropriate when:

---

[3] 12 USC 1828(x), added as part of the Financial Services Regulatory Relief Act of 2006 provides that "(t)he submission by any person of any information to any Federal banking agency, State banking supervisor, or foreign banking authority for any purpose in the course of any supervisory or regulatory process of such agency, supervisor, or authority shall not be construed as waiving, destroying, or otherwise affecting any privilege such person may claim with respect to such information under Federal or State law as to any person or entity other than such agency, supervisor, or authority."

- The bank does not offer residential products or there are few racial or national origin group residents in the bank's market area;
- A comparative file review of any residential product (or of racial or national origin groups) would not be useful and reliable;
- Previous examinations of residential products (or of possible discrimination against racial or national origin groups) have not found any violations or weaknesses in the bank's compliance program; or
- Examiners suspect discrimination in a specific nonresidential product (or on a different prohibited basis).

Examiners should be alert for the presence of conditions that may make it appropriate or necessary to shift the scope or approach of the planned examination, including:

- Insufficient volume of applications to conduct a comparative analysis.
- Sufficient volume of applications to permit comparative analysis by statistical modeling.
- The credit decision maker's lack of knowledge of the prohibited basis identities of customers.

This booklet contains further guidance on these matters at appropriate points. Additionally, appendix M contains a description of alternative fair lending analyses that may be appropriate when reviewing credit card products or banks with an insufficient number of applications that render a comparative file review meaningless.

Key elements of scoping — for example, the prohibited basis, decision center, market, product, and review period — often are identified as part of the OCC's fair lending screening process. Therefore, the scoping procedures in this booklet typically are not applicable to the banks identified in the screening process. However, for examinations of randomly selected banks and banks identified by the supervisory office that are not on the screening lists, examiners should use the scoping procedures. If the supervisory office or OCC policy has designated certain banks, products, market areas, etc., as priorities to examine, OCC examiners should make scoping decisions accordingly.

Examiners typically plan to examine only one focal point. (In certain circumstances, it may be appropriate to examine more than one focal point.)

The focal point includes only one prohibited basis group and one control group at a time to isolate prohibited factors. (For example, compare "black" with "white," not "minority" with "white;" and compare "male" with "female," or "married" with "unmarried," not "married minority female" with "single white male.") The fact that one group outnumbers another in the population or customer pool is not a determinative factor.

After selecting the focal point(s) for review, examiners determine the breadth and depth of the analysis that will be conducted for the selected loan product(s). This process requires a more complete analysis of the bank's compliance risk management process, particularly as it relates to the selected products. Examiners decide on the number of files to review in any transactional analyses performed and whether certain aspects of the credit process deserve heightened scrutiny.

The compliance management process review objective on pages 35 and 36 of this booklet guides examiners in determining the breadth and depth of the examination. There is naturally some interdependence between setting the scope and determining the breadth and depth of the examination. Ultimately both determine the record of performance that serves as the foundation for the OCC's conclusions about bank compliance with fair lending obligations. Examiners employ these procedures and guidelines to arrive at a well-reasoned and practical approach for conducting the fair lending examination.

OCC information on priorities and risks for planning an upcoming examination may expedite the scoping process and make it unnecessary to carry out all of the following steps. For example, the report of the previous fair lending examination may have included recommendations for the focus of the next examination. However, examiners validate that the bank's operational structure, product offerings, and risks have remained the same before adjusting the scoping process.

Examiners use available information and guidance whenever possible to expedite planning and reduce burden on the bank. The OCC resources for determining the focal points worthwhile to examine include:

- Screening data and criteria.
- The OCC or supervisory office priorities.
- The supervisory strategy for the bank.
- Community Reinvestment Act (CRA) performance evaluations.
- Information from community contacts.

- Consumer complaints.
- Home Mortgage Disclosure Act (HMDA), or Fair Housing Home Loan Data System (FHHLDS) data analyses, and other demographic analyses (for example, CRA analyses).

The scoping process can be performed either off-site, onsite, or both, depending on what is most feasible. Any off-site information requests should be made in advance of the on-site examination to permit bank management adequate time to assemble necessary information and provide it to the examination team. (See appendix F, "Potential Scoping Information," for guidance on additional information that examiners might wish to consider, including in a request.)

Examiners select loan products for review and determine the extent of analysis based on:

- An understanding of the bank's credit operations.
- The risk that discriminatory conduct may occur in each area of those operations.
- The feasibility of developing a factually reliable record of a bank's performance and fair lending compliance in each area of those operations.
- Whether the bank has performed any self-evaluation or self-test that could streamline the examination.

Objective: Gain an Understanding of Credit Operations

1. **Before evaluating the potential for discriminatory conduct, review sufficient information about the bank and its market(s) to understand its credit operations and the representation of prohibited basis groups within those markets. The level of detail to be obtained at this stage should be sufficient to identify whether any of the risk factors in the steps below are present. Relevant background information includes:**

- The types and terms of credit products offered, differentiating among broad categories of credit, such as residential, consumer, or commercial as well as product variations within such categories (fixed vs. variable, etc.).
- The volume of, or growth in, lending for each of the credit products offered.

- Whether the bank has a special purpose credit program or other program that is specially designed to assist certain underserved populations.
- The demographics (i.e., race and national origin) of the credit markets in which the bank is doing business.
- The bank's organization of its credit decision-making process, including identification of the delegation of separate lending authorities and the extent to which discretion in pricing or setting credit terms and conditions is delegated to various levels of managers, employees, or independent brokers or dealers.
- The bank's loan officer compensation program.
- The types of relevant documentation/data that are available for loan products and the relative quantity, quality, and accessibility of such information (i.e., for which loan product(s) will the information available be most likely to support a sound and reliable fair lending analysis).
- The extent to which information requests can be readily organized and coordinated with other compliance examination components to reduce undue burden on the bank. (Do not request more information than the examination team can be expected to use during the anticipated course of the examination.)

2. **Recognize that the bank's markets may or may not coincide with its Community Reinvestment Act (CRA) assessment area(s). When appropriate, review the demographics for a broader geographic area than the assessment area.**

3. **When a bank has multiple underwriting or loan processing centers or subsidiaries, each with fully independent credit-granting authority, consider evaluating each center and subsidiary separately, provided a sufficient number of applications or loans exist to support a meaningful analysis. In determining the scope of the examination for such banks, consider whether:**

- Subsidiaries should be examined. The OCC holds a bank responsible for violations by its direct subsidiaries, but not typically for those by its affiliates (unless the affiliate has acted as the agent for the bank or the violation by the affiliate was known or should have been known to the bank before it became involved in the transaction or purchased the affiliate's loans). When seeking to determine a bank's relationship with affiliates that are not supervised financial institutions, there is no legal impediment to seeking information from the affiliate to understand its relationship to the bank. However, if affiliate information appears necessary, discuss that possibility with the supervisory office.

- The underwriting standards and procedures used in the entity being reviewed are used in related entities not scheduled for the planned examination. This helps examiners to recognize the potential scope of policy-based violations.

- The portfolio consists of applications from a purchased institution. If so, for scoping purposes, consider the applications as if the purchasing bank made them. However, for comparison purposes, applications evaluated under the purchased institution's standards are not compared with applications evaluated under the purchasing bank's standards.

- The portfolio includes purchased loans. If so, look for indications that the bank specified loans to purchase based on a prohibited factor or caused a prohibited factor to influence the origination process.

- A complete decision can be made at one of the several underwriting or loan processing centers, each with independent authority. In such a situation, it is best to conduct on-site a separate comparative analysis at each underwriting center. If covering multiple centers is not feasible during the planned examination, review one during the planned examination and review the bank's processes and internal controls to determine whether expanding the scope and/or length of the examination is justified.

- Decision-making responsibility for a single transaction may involve more than one underwriting center. For example, a bank may have authority to decline mortgage applicants, but only the mortgage company subsidiary may approve them. In such a situation, learn which standards are applied in each entity and the location of records needed for the planned comparisons.

- Applicants can be steered from the bank to a subsidiary or other lending channel and vice versa, and what policies and procedures exist to monitor this practice.

- Any third parties, such as brokers or contractors, are involved in the credit decision and how responsibility is allocated among them and the bank. The bank's familiarity with third-party actions may be important, for a bank may be in violation if it participates in transactions in which it knew or reasonably ought to have known other parties were discriminating.

When assessing the bank's own lending operations, understand any dealings the bank has with affiliated and non-affiliated mortgage loan brokers and other third-party lenders.

These brokers may generate mortgage applications and originations solely for a specific bank or may broadly gather loan applications for local, regional, or national lenders. Recognize the impact of these mortgage brokers and other third-party lender actions and application processing operations on the lending operations of the bank. Evaluate broker activity and fair lending compliance related to underwriting, terms and conditions, redlining, and steering, each of which is covered in more depth in other sections of these procedures, regardless of whether the brokers are located in or out of the bank's primary lending or CRA assessment areas.

If the bank is large and geographically diverse, select only as many markets or underwriting centers as can be reviewed readily in depth, rather than selecting proportionally to cover every market. As needed, narrow the focus to the Metropolitan Statistical Area (MSA) or underwriting center(s) that are determined to present the highest discrimination risk. Use the Home Mortgage Disclosure Act Loan Application Register (HMDA-LAR) data organized by underwriting center, if available. After calculating denial rates between the control and prohibited basis groups for the underwriting centers, select the centers with the highest fair lending risk. This approach is also used when reviewing pricing or other terms and conditions of approved applicants from the prohibited basis and control groups. If underwriting centers have fewer than five racial or national origin group denials, do not examine for racial or national origin discrimination in underwriting. Instead, shift the focus to other loan products, prohibited bases, or examination types.

Objective: Consider the Effect of Low-Volume or High-Volume Focal Points

The volume of prohibited basis group applications for the focal point serves as one general indicator of risk, because it represents the number of consumers potentially exposed to illegal discrimination. Other indicators of risk are the presence of the risk factors identified during scoping and the compliance management system review.

In most cases, do not attempt a comparative analysis for a focal point if the numbers of prohibited basis group or control group applications for that focal point during the 12-month period to be reviewed do not meet the minimums in the fair lending sample size tables in appendix D, as follows:

- At least five denied applications from the prohibited basis group and 20 approved applications from the control group for a comparison of approve/deny decisions.
- At least five approved applications from the prohibited basis group and 20 control group approvals for a comparison of pricing, terms, and/or conditions.

If the focal point first selected does not have such volume, a higher-volume focal point generally is chosen for review. When there are not enough applications for comparison by race, national origin, or gender, consider evaluating possible marital status discrimination by comparing married co-applicants with unmarried co-applicants.

When identifying other risk indicators that favor analyzing a prohibited basis group with fewer transactions than the minimum in the sample size tables, consult the supervisory office and, if appropriate, the Compliance Policy Division on possible alternative methods of analysis. For example, there is strong reason to examine a pattern in which almost all of 19 male borrowers received low rates but almost all of four female borrowers received high rates, even though the number of each group is fewer than the stated minimum. Similarly, there would be strong reason to examine a pattern in which almost all of 100 white applicants were approved but all four black applicants were not, even though the number of prohibited basis denials was fewer than five.

If the volume of applications is large, using the OCC's statistical modeling program for the comparative file analysis may be preferable to judgmental comparison and interpretation.

To determine whether the comparative file analysis should be conducted using statistical modeling, take the following steps before setting the scope of an examination.

1. Determine whether:

- The bank reports HMDA (or collects FHHLDS) data on any focal point being considered as the possible scope of the examination.
- The bank's HMDA-Loan Application Register (LAR) is automated and updated through the most recent quarter (as required by Regulation C).

2. Determine whether there were at least 50 control group approvals, 50 control group denials, and 50 prohibited basis group approvals and 50 prohibited basis group denials from the same racial or national origin group during the most recent 12-month period for which the data in step 1 are available, for any single HMDA product in any one decision center of the bank to be examined.

3. If both conditions in step 1 and the condition in step 2 exist, consult the supervisory office and, if appropriate, the Compliance Policy Division about whether a statistical model might be used for the examination. If it is concluded that a statistical model is needed, the supervisory office should contact the Compliance Risk Analysis Division (Compliance RAD) for assistance.

Compliance RAD may request examiners to:

- Obtain the bank's HMDA data in electronic form for all HMDA-reporting decision centers and subsidiaries and all products for the 12-month period for the institution to be examined. The bank's HMDA data and HMDA-LAR are preferable to the HMDA public access tapes, since they are likely to have more recent data.
- Determine how much, if any, of the additional application data (over and above that on the HMDA-LAR) evaluated by the bank's underwriters is maintained by the bank in electronic format for each HMDA product at each HMDA reporter (or other lending entity), and the process and time frame by which the bank might provide such data to the OCC.
- Determine whether the transactions recorded on the HMDA-LAR for the 12-month period include classes of transactions that were underwritten to different standards (for example, for different reporters/entities/decision centers, for different loan purchasers, for an affordable housing product, or according to the standards of an acquiring or acquired institution), and whether those classes can be sorted in the electronic database.

- Provide recommendations regarding how to aggregate, disaggregate, sort, or otherwise analyze the HMDA data (and any additional data), and about which decision centers, products, etc., might be of greatest interest.
- Determine whether and when underwriting standards changed during the 12-month period for any class of transactions.
- Identify bank staff that can interpret the data.
- Determine the dates of projected examination activity and address any other administrative planning issues.

Objective: Evaluate the Potential for Discriminatory Conduct

1. Develop an Overview

No single examination can reasonably be expected to evaluate every prohibited basis, every product, or every underwriting center or subsidiary of a bank. In addition to information gained in the process detailed above, keep in mind the following factors when selecting products for the scoping review:

- The products and prohibited bases that were reviewed during the most recent prior examination(s) and, conversely, the products and prohibited bases that have not recently been reviewed.
- The prohibited basis groups that make up a significant portion of the bank's market for the different credit products offered.
- The products and prohibited basis groups the bank reviewed using either a self-test or a self-evaluation.

Based on consideration of the foregoing factors, request information for all residential and other loan products considered appropriate for scoping the examination. In addition, when feasible, conduct preliminary interviews with the bank's key underwriting personnel and those involved with establishing the bank's pricing policies and practices. Consider and evaluate:

- Underwriting guidelines, policies, and standards.
- Descriptions of credit scoring systems, including a list of factors scored, cutoff scores, extent of validation, and any guidance for handling overrides and exceptions. (Refer to part A of appendix B, "Considering Automated Underwriting and Credit Scoring Risk Factors," for guidance.)
- Applicable pricing policies, risk-based pricing models, and guidance for exercising discretion over loan terms and conditions.

- Descriptions of any compensation system, including whether compensation is related to loan production or pricing.
- The bank's formal and informal relationships with any finance companies, subprime mortgage or consumer lending entities, or similar institutions.
- Loan application forms.
- HMDA-LAR or loan registers and lists of declined applications.
- Description(s) of databases maintained for loan product(s) to be reviewed, especially any record of exceptions to underwriting guidelines.
- Records detailing policy exceptions or overrides, exception reporting, and monitoring processes.
- Copies of any consumer complaints alleging discrimination and related loan files. (Consumer complaints the OCC receives can be accessed via the OCC's CAGWizard.)
- Compliance program materials (particularly fair lending policies), training manuals, organization charts, as well as record keeping and any monitoring protocols, and internal controls.
- Copies of any available marketing materials, descriptions of current or previous marketing plans or programs, or pre-screened solicitations.

If the credit decision makers do not know whether the applicants are in the prohibited basis group or the control group, a comparative file review probably is not appropriate. Therefore, identify:

- The points in the application or underwriting process at which there are face-to-face meetings with applicants; and
- Which of the bank's participants in the credit decision process review or have access to documents with government monitoring information.

The OCC assumes that if any bank employee knows an applicant's race, gender, etc., the bank's credit decision makers have such knowledge, unless specific facts show otherwise.

2. Identify Compliance Program Discrimination Risk Factors

The bank's own compliance program and previous examination findings may indicate system weaknesses that could lead to discrimination. Therefore, review information from examination work papers, bank records, and any available discussions with management representatives in sufficient detail to understand the organization, staffing, training, record keeping, auditing, and policies and procedures of the bank's fair lending compliance systems. Review these systems and consider the following risk factors (factors are numbered alphanumerically to coincide with the type of factor, e.g., "C" for compliance program, "O" for "overt," and "P" for "pricing".).

C1. Overall bank compliance record is weak.
C2. Prohibited basis monitoring information required by applicable law and regulation is nonexistent or incomplete.
C3. Data and/or record keeping problems compromised reliability of previous examination reviews.
C4. Fair lending problems were previously found in one or more bank products or in bank subsidiaries.
C5. The size, scope, and quality of the compliance management program, including senior management's involvement, designation of a compliance officer, and staffing are materially inferior to those of programs customarily found in banks of similar size, market demographics, and credit complexity.
C6. The bank has not updated compliance policies and procedures to reflect changes in law or in agency guidance.
C7. Fair lending training is nonexistent or weak.

Consider these risk factors and their impact on particular lending products and practices as when conducting the product-specific risk review during the scoping steps that follow. When this review identifies fair lending compliance system deficiencies, consider them as part of the compliance management review.

3. Review Residential Loan Products

Although home mortgages may not be the ultimate subject of every fair lending examination, this product line is at least considered when scoping every bank that is engaged in the residential lending market.

Divide home mortgage loans into the following groupings: home purchase, home improvements, and refinancings. Subdivide those three groups further if a bank does a significant number of any of the following types or forms of residential lending, and consider them separately as follows:

- Government-insured loans.
- Mobile home or factory housing loans.
- Wholesale, indirect, and brokered loans.

- Portfolio lending (including portfolios of Fannie Mae/Freddie Mac rejections).

If no specific risk factors point toward selecting a particular loan type/purpose as defined in HMDA, conventional home purchase loans are the first priority, followed by conventional home-improvement loans, government-insured home purchase loans, government-insured home-improvement loans, conventional refinancings, government-insured refinancings, and multifamily loans.

In addition, determine whether the bank offers any conventional "affordable" housing loan programs, special purpose credit programs, or other programs specifically designed to assist certain applicants, such as underserved populations, and whether their terms and conditions make them incompatible with regular conventional loans for comparative purposes. If so, consider them separately.

If previous examinations have demonstrated the following, limit the focus of the current examination to underwriting or processing centers or to other residential products that have received less scrutiny in the past:

- A strong fair lending compliance program.
- No record of discriminatory transactions at particular decision centers or in particular residential products.
- No indication of a significant change in personnel, operations, underwriting standards, or pricing policies at those centers or in those residential products.
- No unresolved fair lending complaints, administrative proceedings, litigation, or similar factors.
- No discretion to set price or credit terms and conditions in particular decision centers or for particular residential products.

4. Identify Residential Lending Discrimination Risk Factors

- Review the lending policies, marketing plans, underwriting, appraisal and pricing guidelines, broker/agent agreements, and loan application forms for each residential loan product that represents an appreciable volume of, or displays noticeable growth in, the bank's residential lending.

Broker/agent agreements and other information about third parties are reviewed to learn the bank's degree of control over, and the level of familiarity with, those activities, its potential legal liability, and any other supervisory risks. The facts of specific relationships will indicate whether the bank may be liable for any discrimination in such activities or in transactions that involve those third parties. Under Regulation B, a bank may be liable for violations committed by another creditor in connection with the same credit transaction if the bank knew or had reasonable notice of the violation before becoming involved in the credit transaction. Consult OCC district counsel to determine whether the bank may be held responsible for the transactions conducted by other creditors.

- Review any available data regarding the geographic distribution of the bank's loan originations with respect to the race and national origin percentages of the census tracts within its assessment area or, if different, its residential loan product lending area(s).

- Conduct interviews of loan officers and other employees or agents in the residential lending process concerning adherence to and understanding of the above policies and guidelines as well as any relevant operating practices. (See the "Underwriter Interview Guide" in appendix J.)

In conducting the foregoing, look for the following risk factors. If any of these risk factors are found, document them and follow-up as called for in the Examination Procedures for Assessing Fair Lending Performance.

NOTE: For risk factors below that are marked with an asterisk (*), examiners need not attempt to calculate the indicated ratios for racial or national origin characteristics when the bank is not a HMDA reporter. However, consider whether such calculations should be made based on sexual, racial, or ethnic surrogates.

OVERT indicators of discrimination, such as:

O1. Including explicit prohibited basis identifiers in the bank's written or oral policies and procedures (underwriting criteria, pricing standards, etc).
O2. Collecting information, conducting inquiries, or imposing conditions contrary to express requirements of Regulation B.
O3. Including variables in a credit scoring system that constitute a basis or factor prohibited by Regulation B or, for residential loan scoring systems, the FH Act. (If a credit scoring system scores age, refer to part E of

appendix B, "Considering Automated Underwriting and Credit Scoring Risk Factors."

O4. Statements made by the bank's officers, employees, or agents which constitute an express or implicit indication that one or more such persons have engaged or do engage in discrimination on a prohibited basis in any aspect of a credit transaction.

O5. Employee or bank statements that evidence attitudes based on prohibited basis prejudices or stereotypes.

Indicators of potential disparate treatment in UNDERWRITING, such as:

U1. *Substantial disparities among the approval/denial rates for applicants by monitored prohibited basis characteristic (especially within income categories).

U2. *Substantial disparities among the application processing times for applicants by monitored prohibited basis characteristic (especially within denial reason groups).

U3. *Substantially higher proportion of withdrawn/incomplete applications from prohibited basis group applicants than from other applicants.

U4. Vague or unduly subjective underwriting criteria.

U5. Lack of clear guidance on making exceptions to underwriting criteria, including credit scoring overrides.

U6. Lack of clear loan file documentation of reasons for any exceptions to standard underwriting criteria, including credit scoring overrides.

U7. Relatively high percentages of either exceptions to underwriting criteria or overrides of credit score cutoffs.

U8. Loan officer or broker compensation based on loan volume (especially loans approved per period of time).

U9. Consumer complaints alleging discrimination in loan processing or in approving/denying residential loans.

Indicators of potential disparate treatment in PRICING (interest rates, fees, or points), such as:

P1. Bank incentives for loan officers or brokers to charge higher prices (including interest rate, fees, and points). Special attention should be given to situations when financial incentives are accompanied by broad pricing discretion (as in P2), such as through the use of overages or yield spread premiums.

P2. Presence of broad discretion in loan pricing (including interest rate, fees, and points), such as through overages, underages, or yield spread premiums. Such discretion may be present even when banks provide rate sheets and fee schedules, if loan officers or brokers deviate from those rates and fees without clear and objective criteria.

P3. Use of risk-based pricing that is not based on objective criteria or applied consistently.

P4. *Substantial disparities among prices being quoted or charged to applicants who differ as to their monitored prohibited basis characteristics.

P5. Consumer complaints alleging discrimination in residential loan pricing.

P6. In mortgage pricing, disparities in the incidence of rate spreads of higher-priced loans by prohibited basis characteristics as reported in the HMDA data (Regulation C, 12 CFR 203.4(a)(12)).

P7. *A loan program that contains only borrowers from a prohibited basis group, or has significant differences in the percentages of prohibited basis groups, especially in the absence of a Special Purpose Credit Program under the ECOA.

Be alert for indications of risk related to other terms or conditions (such as co-signors, collateral, or length of term). For example, broad discretion and vague standards for collateral are viewed as risk factors if they exist for a focal point. Adapt transaction comparison techniques to examine such situations.

In addition, the following are abusive (or "predatory") lending practices that may involve violations of fair lending laws and that the OCC treats as risk factors:[4]

- Collateral or equity "stripping" — loans made in reliance on the liquidation value of the borrower's home or other collateral, rather than the borrower's independent ability to repay, with the possible or even intended result of foreclosure or the need to refinance under duress;
- Interest rates or fees that far exceed the true risk and cost of making the loan;
- Inadequate disclosure of the true costs and risks of loan transactions;
- Lending practices that are fraudulent, coercive, unfair, deceptive, or otherwise illegal;
- Loan terms and structures, such as negative amortization, when designed to make it more difficult or impossible for borrowers to reduce their indebtedness;

---

[4] Evidence of these factors may also represent noncompliance with the OCC Guidelines for Residential Mortgage Lending Practices, Appendix C of 12 CFR 30.

- "Padding" or "packing" — charging customers unearned, concealed, or unwarranted fees;
- "Balloon" payment loans that may conceal the true burden of the loan financing and may force borrowers into costly refinancing or foreclosure situations;
- "Flipping" — frequent and multiple refinancings, usually of mortgage loans, requiring additional fees which strip equity from the borrower;
- Collection of up-front single-premium credit insurance — for example, life, disability, or unemployment insurance — when the consumer does not receive a net tangible financial benefit.

Indicators of potential disparate treatment by STEERING, such as:

S1. Lack of clear, objective, and consistently applied standards for (1) referring applicants to subsidiaries, affiliates, or lending channels within the bank, (2) classifying applicants as "prime" or "subprime" borrowers, or (3) deciding what kinds of alternative loan products should be offered or recommended to applicants (product placement).

S2. Financial incentives for loan officers or brokers to place applicants in nontraditional products (i.e., negative amortization, interest only, or payment option adjustable rate mortgages) or higher cost products.

S3. *For a bank that offers different products based on credit risk levels, any significant differences in percentages of prohibited basis groups in each of the alternative loan product categories.

S4. *Significant differences in the percentage of prohibited basis group applicants in loan products or products with specific features relative to control group applicants. Special attention is given to products and features that have potentially negative consequences for applicants (i.e., non-traditional mortgages, prepayment penalties, lack of escrow requirements, or credit life insurance).

S5. *For a bank that has one or more subprime mortgage subsidiaries or affiliates, any significant differences, by loan product, in the percentage of prohibited basis group applicants of the bank compared with the percentage of prohibited basis group applicants of the subsidiary(ies) or affiliate(s).

S6. *For a bank that has one or more lending channels that originate the same loan product, any significant differences in the percentage of prohibited basis group applicants in one of the lending channels compared with the percentage of prohibited basis group applicants in the other lending channel.

S7. Consumer complaints alleging discrimination in residential loan pricing or product placement.

S8. *For a bank with subprime mortgage subsidiaries, a concentration of those subsidiaries' branches in particular racial or national origin geographic areas relative to its other branches.

In addition, the following may involve violations of fair lending laws, and the OCC treats them as risk factors:

- One-way referrals — for example, a prime lender refers subprime applicants to its subprime subsidiary but the subprime subsidiary does not refer prime applicants to the prime lender; or
- Significant differences in the proportion of loans made predominantly in particular racial or national origin geographic areas between a prime lender and its subprime subsidiary.

Indicators of potential **DISCRIMINATORY REDLINING,** such as:

R1. *Significant differences, as revealed in HMDA data, in the number of applications received, withdrawn, approved not accepted, and closed for incompleteness or loans originated in those areas in the bank's market that have relatively high concentrations of residents of a particular racial or national origin group compared with areas with relatively low concentrations of residents of such racial or national origin group.

R2. *Significant differences between approval/denial rates for all applicants in areas with relatively high concentrations of residents of a particular racial or national origin group compared with areas with relatively low concentrations of residents of such racial or national origin group.

R3. *Significant differences between denial rates based on insufficient collateral for applicants from areas with relatively high concentrations of residents of a particular racial or national origin group and those areas with relatively low concentrations of residents of such racial or national origin group.

R4. *Significant differences in the number of originations of higher-priced loans or loans with potentially negative consequences for borrowers (e.g., non-traditional mortgages, prepayment penalties, lack of escrow requirements) in areas with relatively high concentrations of residents of a particular racial or national origin group compared with areas with relatively low concentrations of residents of such racial or national origin group.

R5. Other patterns of lending identified during the most recent CRA examination that differ by the concentration of residents of a particular racial or national origin group.

R6. Explicit demarcation of credit product markets that excludes metropolitan statistical areas (MSAs), political subdivisions, census tracts, or other geographic areas within the bank's lending market or CRA assessment areas and having relatively high concentrations of residents of a particular racial or national origin group.

R7. Difference in services available or hours of operation at branch offices located in areas with concentrations of residents of a particular racial or national origin group when compared with branch offices located in areas with low concentrations of residents of such racial or national origin group.

R8. Policies on receipt and processing of applications, pricing, conditions, or appraisals and valuation or on any other aspect of providing residential credit that vary between areas with relatively high concentrations of residents of a particular racial or national origin group and those areas with relatively low concentrations of residents of such racial or national origin group.

R9. The bank CRA assessment area(s) appears to have been drawn to exclude areas with relatively high concentrations of residents of a particular racial or national origin group.

R10. Employee statements that reflect an aversion to doing business in areas with relatively high concentrations of residents of a particular racial or national origin group.

R11. Complaints or other allegations by consumers or community representatives that the bank excludes or restricts access to credit for areas with relatively high concentrations of residents of a particular racial or national origin.

Review complaints against the bank filed with the OCC's Customer Assistance Group (CAG); the CRA public comment file; community contact forms; and responses to questions about redlining, discrimination, and discouragement of applications, and about meeting the needs of racial or national origin minorities, asked as part of "obtaining local perspectives on the performance of financial lenders" during prior CRA examinations.

> **NOTE:** Broad allegations or complaints are not, by themselves, sufficient justification to shift the focus of an examination from routine comparative review of applications to redlining analysis. Such a shift should be based on complaints or allegations of specific practices or

incidents that are consistent with redlining, along with the existence of other risk factors.

R12. A bank that has most of its branches in neighborhoods predominantly composed of a particular racial or national origin group at the same time that the bank's subprime mortgage subsidiary has branches located primarily in neighborhoods that are not predominantly composed of such racial or national origin group.

Indicators of potential **DISPARATE TREATMENT IN MARKETING** of residential products, such as:

M1. Advertising patterns or practices that a reasonable person would believe indicate prohibited basis customers are less desirable.

M2. Advertising only in media serving particular racial or national origin areas of the market.

M3. Marketing through brokers or other agents that the bank knows (or has reason to know) would serve only one racial or national origin group in the market.

M4. Use of marketing programs or procedures for residential loan products that exclude one or more regions or geographies within the bank's assessment or marketing area that have significantly higher percentages of residents of a particular racial or national origin group than does the remainder of the assessment or marketing area.

M5. Using mailing or other distribution lists or other marketing techniques for pre-screened or other offerings of residential loan products that exclude:

- Explicitly groups of prospective borrowers on a prohibited basis; or
- Geographies (e.g., census tracts and ZIP codes) within the bank's marketing area that have significantly higher percentages of residents of a particular racial or national origin group than does the remainder of the marketing area.

M6. *Proportion of monitored prohibited basis applicants is significantly lower than that group's representation in the total population of the market area.

M7. Consumer complaints alleging discrimination in advertising or marketing loans.

In addition, the following are lending practices that may involve violations of fair lending laws and that the OCC treats as risk factors:

- Targeting persons, such as the elderly, women, minorities, and persons living in low- or moderate-income areas, who are perceived to be less financially sophisticated or otherwise vulnerable to abusive loan practices;
- Aggressive marketing tactics that amount to deceptive or coercive conduct.

Indicators of potential disparate treatment in **LOAN SERVICING AND LOSS MITIGATION,** such as:

L1. *Substantial disparities among loss mitigation servicing options by prohibited basis group characteristic.

L2. *Substantial disparities in decision processing times by prohibited basis group characteristic.

L3. *Significant disparities in the completion of foreclosure actions once legal process initiated by prohibited basis group characteristic.

L4. Lack of clear loan file documentation for servicing or loss mitigation decisions, granting of policy exceptions, or reasons for fee waivers.

L5. Weak or non-existent process and controls to ensure ongoing fair lending compliance, including that of third-party vendors.

L6. Lack of clear guidance on determining appropriate loss mitigation options, making policy exceptions, or granting fee waivers.

L7. Internal audits, compliance reviews, or monitoring reports identifying significant weaknesses or violations in handling exceptions, fee waivers, incorrect credit reporting agency reporting, or complying with bank policies and procedures.

L8. Consumer complaints alleging discrimination in servicing or loss mitigation practices.

L9. High volume of policy exceptions or fee waivers by prohibited basis group characteristic.

L10. Significant level of litigation alleging discrimination in loan servicing or loss mitigation practices.

L11. Broad employee discretion in determining loan servicing and loss mitigation actions.

L12. Employees collecting information, conducting inquiries, or imposing conditions inconsistent with express Regulation B or FH Act requirements.

L13. Collection practices not based on delinquency status.

L14. Employee compensation based on workout, loss mitigation, or foreclosure strategy adopted.

L15. Lack of clear consumer disclosures on loss mitigation options available, the costs of each option, and the risks involved.

L16. Lack of clear procedures for determining a borrower's ability to repay when selecting loss mitigation options.

L17. Vague or subjective criteria for property inspections, broker price offers, appraisals, or other valuations.

Indicators of potential disparate treatment in **HELOC MODIFICATIONS,** such as:

H1. Significant value decline methodology not clearly supported, objectively determined, or consistently applied.

H2. Process to establish that borrower's financial condition significantly deteriorated beyond ability to repay not reasonable, objectively supportable, or clearly documented.

H3. Soft or deteriorating market determinations not based on reasonable economic criteria, supportable standards, consistently applied, or clearly documented.

H4. Soft or deteriorating market or declining market value determinations not considering potential disparate impact/redlining implications.

H5. Regulation Z, Regulation B, and FCRA adverse action disclosure process, as applicable, is not timely or does not exist.

H6. Under Regulation B, limitations regarding change in marital status, age, or retirement or additional creditworthiness information not considered.

H7. Market area determinations based on ZIP codes or census tracts rather than MSAs or larger geographical subdivisions.

H8. Borrower appeal process on how to initiate an appeal not readily available, consistently provided, or clearly explained.

5. Organize and Focus Residential Risk Factors

Review the risk factors identified in step 4 and, for each loan product that displays risk factors, articulate the possible discriminatory effects encountered, and organize the examination of those loan products in accordance with the following guidance:

- When overt evidence of discrimination, as described in factors O1-O5, has been found in a product, document those findings as described on pages 40 and 41 and complete the remainder of the planned examination analysis.

- When any of the risk factors U1-U9 are present, consider conducting an underwriting comparative file analysis described on pages 41-46.
- When any of the risk factors P1-P7 are present, consider conducting a pricing comparative file analysis as described on pages 46-49.
- When any of the risk factors S1-S8 are present, consider conducting a steering analysis as described on pages 49-54.
- When any of the risk factors R1-R12 are present, consult the supervisory office and, if appropriate, the Compliance Policy Division about conducting an analysis for redlining as described on pages 57-68.
- When any of the risk factors M1-M7 are present, consult the supervisory office and, if appropriate, the Compliance Policy Division about conducting a marketing analysis as described on pages 68-70.
- When any of the risk factors L1-L17 are present, consider conducting a comparative file analysis similar to that described on pages 41-46 or a pricing comparative file review as described on pages 46-49, as appropriate.
- When any of the risk factors H1-H8 are present, consider conducting a comparative file analysis similar to that described on pages 41-46 or a redlining analysis as described on pages 57-68.
- When a bank uses age in any credit scoring system, consider conducting an examination analysis of that credit scoring system's compliance with the requirements of Regulation B as described on page 70.

If one or more compliance-related risk factors exist along with the other risk factors for a focal point, designate that focal point even more strongly for examination.

6. Identify Consumer Lending Discrimination Risk Factors

For any consumer loan products selected in step 1 for risk analysis in the current examination cycle, conduct a risk factor review similar to that conducted for residential lending products in steps 3 through 5, above. Consult the supervisory office and, if appropriate, the Compliance Policy Division about the potential use of surrogates to identify possible prohibited basis group persons.

NOTE: The term surrogate in this context refers to any factor related to a loan applicant that potentially identifies that applicant's race or other prohibited basis characteristic when no direct evidence of that characteristic is available. Thus, in consumer lending, when monitoring data is generally unavailable, a Hispanic or Asian surname could constitute a surrogate for an applicant's race or national origin because examiners can assume that the bank (which can rebut the presumption) perceived the person to be Hispanic or Asian. Similarly, an applicant's given name could serve as a surrogate for his or her gender. A surrogate for a prohibited basis group characteristic may be used to set up a comparative analysis with control group applicants or borrowers.

Using decision rules in steps 3 through 5 above, for residential lending products, identify the possible discriminatory patterns encountered and consider examining those products determined to have sufficient risk of discriminatory conduct.

7. Identify Commercial Lending Discrimination Risk Factors

When a bank lends a substantial amount in the commercial lending market, most notably to small businesses, and the product has not recently been examined or the underwriting standards have changed since the last examination of the product, consider conducting a risk factor review similar to that performed for residential lending products, as feasible, given the limited information available. Such an analysis should generally be limited to determining risk potential based on risk factors U4-U8, P1-P3, R5-R7, and M1-M3.

Focus on small business credit (commercial loan applicants that had gross revenues of $1,000,000 or less in the preceding fiscal year), unless evidence that a concentration on other commercial products is more appropriate.

If the bank makes commercial loans insured by the Small Business Administration (SBA), consult the supervisory office and, if appropriate, the Compliance Policy Division to determine whether SBA loan data (which codes race and other factors) are available for the bank and whether an evaluation of the data is warranted.

For large banks reporting small business loans for CRA purposes and when the bank also voluntarily geocodes loan denials, look for material discrepancies in ratios of approval-to-denial rates for applications in areas with relatively high concentrations of residents of a particular racial or national origin group compared with areas with low concentrations of residents of such racial or national origin group.

Articulate the possible discriminatory patterns identified and consider further examining those products that have sufficient risk of discriminatory conduct in accordance with commercial lending procedures described on pages 54-57.

Objective: Determine the reliability of the bank's compliance management process and use the findings to adjust the examination scope.

The quality of the bank's compliance management processes for ensuring compliance with fair lending laws and regulations and identifying fair lending problems affects how examiners sample and review individual loan decisions.

1. **Determine whether the bank's policies and procedures enable management to prevent, or to identify and self-correct, illegal disparate treatment in the transactions that relate to the products and issues identified for further analysis during the Examination Procedures for Setting the Examination Scope phase of these procedures.**

2. **Obtain a thorough understanding of the manner by which management addresses its fair lending responsibilities for (a) the bank's lending practices and standards, (b) training and other application-processing aids, (c) guidance to employees or agents in dealing with customers, and (d) its marketing or other promotion of products and services.**

3. **Consider bank records and interviews with appropriate management personnel in the lending, compliance, audit, and legal functions. Also refer to the "Compliance Management Analysis Checklist" in appendix A to evaluate the strength of the compliance programs in terms of their capacity to prevent, or to identify and self-correct, fair lending violations in the products or issues selected for analysis. Based on this evaluation:**

   - Minimize sample sizes within the guidelines established in the "Fair Lending Sample Size Tables" in appendix D, to the extent warranted by the strength and thoroughness of the compliance programs applicable to focal points selected for examination. For focal points at banks selected through the OCC's risk-based screening process, complete the checklist but select the largest sample sizes within the ranges corresponding to the volumes of applications for the focal point, unless the compliance management review resolves concerns about the specific indications of risk that caused the bank to be selected for examination.

- Identify any compliance program or system deficiencies that merit correction or improvement and present these to management as part of concluding the examination.

When a bank performs a self-evaluation or a self-test of any product or issue that is within the examination scope, streamline the examination, consistent with the requirements set forth in appendix H, "Using Self-Tests and Self-Evaluations to Streamline the Examination."

Objective: Complete the Examination Scoping Process

1. **Review the results of the preceding objectives and select those focal points that warrant examination, based on the relative risk levels identified above. Depending on the overall supervisory strategy and available resources, choose a smaller number of focal points from among all those selected on the basis of risk. In such instances, set the scope by first prioritizing focal points on the basis of (1) high number and/or relative severity of risk factors; (2) high data quality and other factors affecting the likelihood of obtaining reliable examination results; (3) high loan volume and the likelihood of widespread risk to applicants and borrowers; and (4) low quality of any compliance program. Then select for examination as many focal points as resources permit.**

   When the judgment process among competing focal points is a close call, information learned in the phase of conducting the compliance management review can be used to further refine the examiner's choices.

2. **Once the scope has been set, send the bank a request letter (see sample fair lending section of request letter in appendix I). The letter should state that the examination may be streamlined if the bank conducted any self-evaluations on the transactions within the proposed scope of the examination. Evaluate these self-evaluations as called for in "Using Self-Tests and Self-Evaluations to Streamline the Examination" in appendix H.**

Examination Procedures for Assessing Fair Lending Performance

Once the loan product(s) and the extent of file review for the examination have been determined, assess the bank's fair lending performance by applying the appropriate procedures that follow to each of the selected examination focal points.

If the bank was selected for examination through the OCC's risk-based screening process, proceed with the type of analysis identified as appropriate in the screening process. If the bank was selected for examination through the supervisory office risk assessment process or the OCC's random sample process, apply the appropriate analysis to the identified focal point. The analyses below will not apply if statistical modeling is used.

Objective: Verify Accuracy of Data

Prior to any analysis and preferably before the scoping process, assess the accuracy of the data being reviewed. Data verification should follow specific procedures (sampling size, etc.) intended to ensure the validity of the review. For example, when a bank's HMDA-LAR data is relied upon, validate the accuracy of the bank's submitted data by selecting a sample of HMDA-LAR entries and verify that the information noted on the HMDA-LAR was reported according to instructions by comparing information contained in the loan file for each sampled loan. If the HMDA-LAR data are inconsistent with the information contained in the loan files, depending on the nature of the errors, a fair lending analysis may require postponement until the bank corrects the data on the HMDA-LAR. When inaccuracies impede the examination, direct the bank to take action to ensure data integrity (data scrubbing, monitoring, training, etc.).

NOTE: While the procedures refer to using HMDA data, consider other data sources, especially in the case of non-HMDA reporters or banks that originate loans, but are not required to report them on a HMDA-LAR.

Objective: Document Regulation B Compliance Checklists

If the fair lending examination involves a review of transaction files, record information on two checklists as described below.

1. **Other Illegal Limitations on Credit Checklist.**

   Before reviewing files for the comparative treatment of applicants, review the "Other Illegal Limitations on Credit Checklist" in appendix K to identify possible violations. Note that the bank's policy or conduct does not have to treat applicants differently on a prohibited basis to violate one of those requirements; however, also report whether or not prohibited disparate treatment is indicated with apparent violations of this type. Maintain one master checklist with information about any apparent violations found during the file review. Identify any apparent violations (even isolated), then request explanations from the bank staff responsible for the transactions, evaluate each explanation, and verify any facts relied upon by the bank. If the explanations are not adequate, proceed as directed in procedures for "Concluding the Examination."

2. **Technical Compliance Checklist.**

   Use copies of the "Technical Compliance Checklist" in appendix L to review six files (an approved and a denied consumer, business, and residential real estate loan application file) and note any apparent violations. If violations exist in those six files, then, during the comparative file review for the focal point, observe and note on one master copy of the checklist whether the violations recur in the comparative file review.

Objective: Conduct an Underwriter Interview

Every fair lending examination includes an interview of the decision-making underwriters (or equivalent bank staff, depending on the type of analysis). From these interviews, learn in detail how the credit criteria were applied and how the lending process operated. Use the "Underwriter Interview Guide" in appendix J. Use the underwriter's statements as a framework for the comparisons and for evaluating any explanations offered later by the bank if it is asked to account for potential disparate treatment between the prohibited basis group and control group.

The information obtained from the interview may make it necessary to change the scope or sample composition.

Objective: Document Overt Evidence of Disparate Treatment

When the scoping process or any other examination activity identifies overt evidence of disparate treatment, assess the nature of the policy or statement and the extent of its impact on affected applicants by conducting the following analysis.

1. **When the indicator(s) of overt discrimination are found in, or based on, a written policy (for example, a credit scorecard) or communication, determine and document:**

   a. The precise language of the potentially discriminatory policy or communication and the nature of the fair lending concerns that it raises.
   b. The bank's stated purpose in adopting the policy or communication and the identity of the person on whose authority it was issued or adopted.
   c. How and when the policy or communication was put into effect.
   d. How widely the policy or communication was applied.
   e. Whether and to what extent applicants were adversely affected by the policy or communication.

2. **When any indicator of overt discrimination was an oral statement or unwritten practice, determine and document:**

   a. The precise nature of either the statement or practice and of the fair lending concerns that they raise.
   b. The identity of the persons making the statement or applying the practice and their descriptions of the reasons for it and the persons authorizing or directing the use of the statement or practice.
   c. How and when the statement or practice was disseminated or put into effect.
   d. How widely the statement or practice was disseminated or applied.
   e. Whether and to what extent applicants were adversely affected by the statement or practice.

   After documenting those situations as called for here, request an explanation and evaluate that explanation in light of the guidance on overt evidence of discrimination in "Evaluating Bank Responses to Evidence of Disparate Treatment" in appendix C.

   Assemble findings and supporting documentation for presentation to bank management when concluding the examination.

Objective: Conduct Transactional Underwriting Analysis – Residential and Consumer Loans

Depending on the extent of the file review and the size of the applicant population reviewed, the analysis of underwriting decisions may involve a manual comparative file review, a statistical analysis, or other specialized techniques. Each examination process assesses a bank's credit-decision standards and whether decisions on pricing and other terms and conditions are applied to borrowers without regard to a prohibited basis.

1. **Set Sample Size**

   a. For each focal point being reviewed, select two samples: (1) prohibited basis group denials; and (2) control group approvals. Choose the samples either directly from monitoring information in residential loan applications or through application data and use of surrogates in consumer applications.

   b. Using table A in the "Fair Lending Sample Size Tables," appendix D, determine the initial sample sizes for each focal point, based on the number of prohibited basis group denials and the number of control group approvals during the 12-month (or calendar year) period preceding the examination. If the number of prohibited basis group denials and/or control group approvals during the preceding 12-month period substantially exceeds the maximum sample size shown in table A, reduce the time period from which the samples are selected to a shorter period. (In doing so, try to select a period in which the bank's underwriting standards are most representative of those in effect during the full 12-month period preceding the examination.)

   c. If the number of prohibited basis group denials or control group approvals for a given focal point during the 12-month period referenced in 1.b., above, does not meet the minimum standards set forth in the sample size table, do not conduct a transactional analysis for that focal point. If other risk factors favor analyzing such a focal point, consult the supervisory office and, if appropriate, the Compliance Policy Division on possible alternative methods of judgmental comparative analysis.

   See appendix D for additional guidance on using the sample size tables.

NOTE: Regardless of application volume or sample size, any clear instance of potential disparate treatment — even if the comparison consists of only two files — must be treated as an apparent violation.

2. **Determine Sample Composition**

   a. To the extent the bank maintains records of loan outcomes resulting from exceptions to its credit underwriting standards or other policies (e.g., overrides to credit score cutoffs), request such records for both approvals and denials, sorted by loan product and branch or decision center, if the bank can do so. Include in the initial sample for each focal point all exceptions or overrides applicable to that focal point.

   b. Using HMDA/LAR data or, for consumer loans, comparable loan register data to the extent available, choose approved and denied applications based on selection criteria that maximize the likelihood of finding marginal approved and denied applicants, as discussed below.

   c. To the extent that the above factors are inapplicable or other selection criteria are unavailable or do not facilitate selection of the entire sample size of files, complete the initial sample selection by making random file selections from the appropriate sample categories in the sample size table.

If the sample size is much smaller than the total number of transactions in the period, select the sample based on the following features:

- Applications for residential loans other than "jumbo" loans.
- Approvals with the highest ratio of loan amount sought relative to income.
- Approvals with the longest processing times.
- Denials with the lowest ratio of loan amount sought to income.
- Denials involving questionable circumstances (for example, denial one day after application with the denial reason "unable to verify").

Transactions with the features above are more likely to be "marginal transactions," as defined in step 3 below.

3. **Compare Approved and Denied Applications**

Although a bank's written policies and procedures may appear to be nondiscriminatory, lending personnel may interpret or apply policies in a discriminatory manner. To detect any disparate treatment among applicants, first eliminate all but "marginal transactions" (see 3.b. below) from each selected focal point sample. Then, record on an applicant profile spreadsheet a detailed description of each marginal applicant's qualifications, the level of assistance received during the application process, the reasons for denial, the loan terms, and other information. Once profiled, compare the prohibited basis and control groups for evidence that similarly qualified applicants have been treated differently as to either the bank's credit decision or the quality of assistance provided.

a. Create Applicant Profile Spreadsheet

- Based upon the bank's written or articulated credit standards and loan policies, create a worksheet or computerized spreadsheet with each applicant's name and each data element to be reviewed. Always include in the spreadsheet certain data elements (income, loan amount, debt, etc.), while the other data selected will be tailored for each loan product and bank based on applicable underwriting criteria and such issues as branch location and underwriter. When credit bureau scores and/or application scores are an element of the bank's underwriting criteria (or when such information is regularly recorded in loan files, whether expressly used or not), include a data field for this information in the spreadsheet.

- To facilitate comparisons of the quality of assistance provided to prohibited basis group and control group applicants, respectively, provide a "comments" block on the worksheet to record observations from the file or interviews about how an applicant was, or was not, assisted in overcoming credit deficiencies or otherwise qualifying for approval.

NOTE: All examiners who review files meet prior to starting the file review to ensure that they have a uniform understanding of the file items to be identified and recorded (for example, how credit report codes will be interpreted, debt ratios will be calculated, and income and monthly loan payments will be totaled).

b. Complete Applicant Profiles

From the application files sample for each focal point, complete applicant profiles for selected denied and approved applications as follows:

A principal goal is to identify when similarly qualified prohibited basis and control group applicants had different credit outcomes, because the agencies have found that discrimination, including differences in granting assistance during the approval process, is more likely to occur for applicants who are *not* either clearly qualified or unqualified, i.e., "marginal" applicants. The examiner-in-charge should, during the following steps, judgmentally select from the initial sample only those denied and approved applications that constitute marginal transactions. (See appendix E "Identifying Marginal Transactions" for guidance.)

- Review denied application files in the sample to eliminate any prohibited basis group applicants with qualifications so weak that there are not likely to be any approved applicants with similar qualifications. Record only the name and/or number of the application, the disposition, and the key facts justifying the credit decision.

- Similarly, review the approved control group application files to eliminate well-qualified control group applicants (those without flaws or with flaws too minor to serve as a basis for denial). Record only the name and/or number of the application, the disposition, and the key facts justifying the credit decision.

- If few marginal control group applicants are identified from the initial sample, review additional files of approved control group applicants. This will either increase the number of marginal approvals or confirm that marginal approvals are so infrequent that the marginal denials are unlikely to involve disparate treatment.

- Perform the judgmental selection of both marginal-denied and marginal-approved applicant loan files together, in a "back and forth" manner, to facilitate close matches and a more consistent definition of "marginal" between these two types of loan files.

- Once the "marginal" applicants are identified, record the applicant data elements for each "marginal" applicant on the worksheet or spreadsheet. When more than one reason for denial exists, but the applicant nearly met the bank's standard for each requirement, retain the denied file in the sample to use in comparisons for each reason.

- While conducting the preceding step, simultaneously look for and document on the spreadsheet any evidence found in marginal files regarding the extent:

  - Of any assistance, including both affirmative aid and waivers or partial waivers of credit policy provisions or requirements, that appears to have been provided to marginal-approved control group applicants which enabled them to overcome one or more credit deficiencies, such as excessive debt-to-income ratios.
  - To which marginal-denied prohibited basis group applicants with similar deficiencies were, or were not, provided similar affirmative aid, waivers, or other forms of assistance.

c. Review and Compare Profiles

- For each focal point, review all marginal profiles to determine if the underwriter followed bank lending policies in denying applications and whether the reason(s) for denial were supported by facts documented in the loan file and properly disclosed to the applicant pursuant to Regulation B. If any (a) unexplained deviations from credit standards, (b) inaccurate reasons for denial, or (c) incorrect disclosures are noted (whether in a judgmental underwriting system, a scored system, or a mixed system), obtain an explanation from the underwriter and document the response on an appropriate work paper.

  NOTE: In constructing the applicant profiles to be compared, select the facts to compare so that assistance, waivers, or acts of discretion are treated consistently between applicants. For example, if a control group applicant's Debt To Income (DTI) ratio was lowered to 42 percent because the bank decided to include short-term overtime income, and a prohibited basis group applicant who was denied due to "insufficient income" would have had his ratio drop from 46 percent to 41 percent if his short-term overtime income had been considered, consider 41 percent, not 46 percent, in determining the benchmark.

- For each reason for denial identified within the target group, rank the denied prohibited basis group applicants, beginning with the applicant whose qualification(s) related to that reason for denial were **least deficient**. (The top-ranked denied applicant in each such ranking will be referred to below as the "benchmark" applicant.)

- Compare each marginal control group approval with the benchmark applicant in each reason-for-denial ranking developed in step (b), above. If there are no approvals who are equally or less qualified, then there are no instances of disparate treatment for the bank to explain. For all such approvals that appear no better qualified than the denied benchmark applicant:

  - Identify the approved applicant on the worksheet or spreadsheet as an "overlap approval," and
  - Compare that overlap approval with other marginal prohibited basis group denials in the ranking to determine whether additional overlaps exist. If so, identify all overlapping approvals and denials as above.

  NOTE: When the focal point involves use of a credit scoring system, the analysis for disparate treatment is similar to the procedures set forth above, and should focus primarily on scoring system overrides. For guidance on this type of analysis, refer to part C of the "Considering Automated Underwriting and Credit Scoring Risk Factors" (appendix B).

4. **Obtain explanations from the appropriate loan officer or other employee for any differences that exist and reanalyze the sample for evidence of discrimination.**

5. **If there is some evidence of violations in the underwriting process but not enough to clearly establish the existence of a pattern or practice, expand the sample as necessary to determine whether a pattern or practice exists. NOTE: A pattern or practice does not have to exist for there to be a violation and possible referral to an enforcement agency.**

6. **Discuss all findings resulting from the above comparisons with bank management and document both the findings and all conversations on an appropriate worksheet.**

Objective: Analyze Potential Disparities in Pricing and Other Terms and Conditions

Depending on the extent of the file review and the size of the borrower population reviewed, the analysis of decisions on pricing and other terms and conditions may involve a manual comparative file review, a statistical analysis, or other specialized techniques. Each examination process assesses a bank's credit-decision standards and whether decisions on pricing and other terms and conditions are applied to borrowers without regard to a prohibited basis.

The procedures below encompass the examination steps for a comparative file review.

1. Set Sample Size

Review data in its entirety or restrict the analysis to a sample depending on the examination approach used and the quality of the bank's compliance management process.

a. For each focal point being reviewed, select two samples: (i) prohibited basis group approvals; and (ii) control group approvals, both identified either directly from monitoring information in residential loan applications or through application data or use of surrogates in consumer or commercial applications.

b. Using table B in the "Fair Lending Sample Size Tables," appendix D, determine the initial sample sizes for each focal point, based on the number of prohibited basis group approvals and the number of control group approvals during the 12-month (or calendar year) period preceding the examination. If the number of prohibited basis group approvals and/or control group approvals during the preceding 12-month period substantially exceeds the maximum sample size shown in table B, reduce the time period from which the samples are selected to a shorter period. (In doing so, select a period in which the bank's standards for the term or condition being reviewed are most representative of those in effect during the full 12-month period preceding the examination.)

NOTE: Regardless of application volume or sample size, any clear instance of potential disparate treatment — even if the comparison consists of only two files — must be treated as an apparent violation.

2. **Determine Sample Composition and Create Applicant Profiles**

   NOTE: Sample composition for a comparison of price and other terms and conditions will initially focus on controlling for two nondiscriminatory variables that can have a significant impact on loan terms: whether the loan was sold and the loan closing date. Other variables, such as household income and loan amount, will be accounted for on a case-by-case basis during the file comparison process.

   a. While the period for review should be 12 months, prohibited basis group and control group approvals should be grouped and reviewed around a range of dates during which the bank's practices for the term or condition being reviewed were the same. Generally, use the loan origination date or approval date for those not accepted by the applicant.

   b. Tailor the sample and subsequent analysis to the specific factors that the bank considers when determining its pricing, terms, and conditions. For example, while decisions on pricing and other terms and conditions are part of the bank's underwriting process, general underwriting criteria should not be used in the analysis if they are not relevant to the term or condition to be reviewed. Additionally, consider only legitimate factors.

   c. Identify data to be analyzed for each focal point to be reviewed and record this information for each approval on a worksheet or computerized spreadsheet to ensure a valid comparison of terms and conditions. For example, in certain cases, a bank may offer slightly differentiated products with significant pricing implications to borrowers. In these cases, group these products together for evaluation.

3. **Compare Terms and Conditions with Applicant Outcomes**

   a. Review all loan terms and conditions (rates, points, fees, maturity variations, loan-to-value (LTV), collateral requirements, etc.), paying special attention to those that are left to the discretion of loan officers or underwriters. For each such term or condition, identify (a) any approved prohibited basis group applicants in the sample who appear to have been treated unfavorably for that term or condition and (b) any approved control group applicants who appear to have been treated favorably for that term or condition. Thoroughly document this analysis in the work papers.

b. Identify from the sample any control group approvals that appear to have been treated more favorably than one or more of the above-identified prohibited basis group approvals and that have negative pricing or creditworthiness factors (under the bank's standards) equal to or less favorable than the prohibited basis group approvals.

4. **Obtain explanations from the appropriate loan officer or other employee for any differences that exist and reanalyze the sample for evidence of discrimination.**

5. **If there is some evidence of violations in the imposition of terms and conditions but not enough to clearly establish the existence of a pattern or practice, expand the sample as necessary to determine whether a pattern or practice exists.**

   NOTE: There does not have to be a pattern or practice to justify a violation and possible referral to an enforcement agency.

6. **Discuss differences in comparable loans with the bank's management and document all conversations on an appropriate worksheet. For additional guidance on evaluating management's responses, refer to part A, 1 - 5, "Evaluating Bank Responses to Evidence of Disparate Treatment" in appendix C.**

Objective: Evaluate Potential for Discriminatory Steering

A bank that offers lending products or product features, either through one channel or through multiple channels, may benefit consumers by offering greater choices and meeting the diverse needs of applicants. Greater product offerings and multiple channels, however, may also create a fair lending risk that applicants will be illegally steered to certain choices based on a prohibited basis.

The following examples illustrate potential fair lending risk:

- A bank that offers different lending products based on credit risk level may enable loan officers or brokers to illegally steer applicants to the higher-risk products.
- A bank that offers nontraditional loan products or loan products with potentially onerous terms (such as prepayment penalties) may enable loan officers or brokers to illegally steer applicants to certain products or features.
- A bank that offers subprime products through different channels may enable applicants to be illegally steered to the subprime channel.

The distinction between guiding consumers toward a specific product or feature and steering, illegal under the fair lending laws, centers on whether the bank did so on a prohibited basis, rather than based on an applicant's needs or other legitimate factors. Examiners need not demonstrate financial harm to a group that has been "steered," but only to demonstrate that that action was taken on a prohibited basis regardless of the financial outcome.

If the scoping analysis reveals the presence of one or more risk factors S1 through S8 for any selected focal point, consult the supervisory office and, if appropriate, the Compliance Policy Division about conducting a steering analysis, as described below.

1. **Clarify what options are available to applicants**

   a. Determine each focal point (product-alternative product pairing or grouping) to be reviewed.

   b. Through interviews with appropriate bank personnel and review of policy manuals, procedure guidelines, and other directives, obtain and verify the following information for each product-alternative product pairing or grouping identified:

   - All underwriting criteria for the product or feature and for their alternatives that the bank, subsidiary, or affiliate offered. Examples of products may include stated income, negative amortization, and option ARMs. Examples of terms and features include prepayment penalties and escrow requirements. The distinction between a product, term, and feature may vary from bank to bank. For example, some banks may consider a "stated income" loan a feature, while others may consider it a distinct product.

- Pricing or other costs applicable to the product and the alternative product(s), including interest rates, points, and all fees.

2. **Document the policies, conditions, or criteria that the bank has adopted for determining how referrals are to be made and choices presented to customers.**

   a. Review any policies and procedures established by the bank and/or the subsidiary or affiliate for (1) referring a person who applies to the bank, but does not meet its criteria, to another internal lending channel, subsidiary, or affiliate; (2) offering one or more alternatives to a person who applies to the bank for a specific product or feature, but does not meet its criteria; (3) referring a person who applies to a subsidiary or affiliate for its product to the bank, when that person appears to be qualified for a loan from the bank; or (4) referring a person who applies for a product through one internal lending channel to another lending channel, when that person appears to be qualified for a loan through the lending channel to which he or she applied.

   Review information about the product or feature offered by the bank and alternative products offered by subsidiaries or affiliates, and information on products and alternatives offered solely by the bank, e.g., conventional and FHA, secured and unsecured home improvement loans, and prime and subprime mortgages.

   b. Obtain any information on a subsidiary of the bank directly from that entity, but seek information on an affiliate or holding company subsidiary only from the bank.

   c. Obtain documentation and/or employee estimates on the volume of referrals made from or to the bank, for each product, during a relevant time period.

   d. Determine whether loan personnel are encouraged, through financial incentives or otherwise, to make referrals, either from the bank to a subsidiary or affiliate or vice versa. Similarly, determine whether the bank provides financial incentives related to products and features.

   e. After reviewing all appropriate documentation, prepare a written summary of all discussions with loan personnel and managers.

f. Resolve to the extent possible any discrepancies between information found in the bank's documents and information obtained in discussions with loan personal and managers by conducting appropriate follow-up interviews.

3. **Determine how referral decisions are made to another lending channel, subsidiary, or affiliate. Determine the reason(s) for referral and how they are documented.**

4. **Determine if individual loan personnel can exercise personal discretion in deciding what loan products or other credit alternatives they will offer a given applicant.**

5. **Determine whether individual decision makers in fact adhere to the bank's stated policies, conditions, or criteria. If not, determine whether different policies or practices are actually in effect.**

   Using the worksheets or computerized spreadsheets developed in step 6 below, record data for the prohibited basis group sample and determine whether the bank is, in fact, applying its criteria as stated. For example, if one announced criterion for receiving a "more favorable" prime mortgage loan was a back-end debt ratio of no more than 38 percent, review the spreadsheets to determine whether that criteria was adhered to. If the bank's actual treatment of prohibited basis group applicants appears to differ from its stated criteria, document such differences for subsequent discussion with management.

6. **To the extent that individual loan personnel have any discretion in deciding the credit products and features to offer applicants, conduct a comparative analysis to determine whether that discretion has been exercised in a nondiscriminatory manner.**

   Compare the bank's, subsidiary's, or affiliate's treatment of control group and prohibited basis group applicants by adapting the "benchmark" and "overlap" technique discussed in these procedures. For purposes of this steering analysis, conduct that technique as follows:

   a. For each focal point to be analyzed, select a sample of prohibited basis group applicants who received "less favorable" treatment (e.g., referral to a finance company or a subprime mortgage subsidiary or counteroffers of less favorable product alternatives).

NOTE: In selecting the sample, follow the guidance of table B in the "Fair Lending Sample Size Tables," appendix D, and select "marginal applicants" as instructed in the Objective: Conduct Transactional Underwriting Analysis – Residential and Consumer Loans.

b. Prepare a spreadsheet for the sample that contains data entry categories for those underwriting and referral criteria the bank identified in the above steps as used in reaching underwriting and referral decisions between the pairs of products.

c. Review the "less favorably" treated prohibited basis group sample and rank this sample from least qualified to best qualified applicant based on the criteria identified for the control group. The best qualified applicant becomes the "benchmark" applicant.

d. Select a sample of control group applicants. Identify those who were treated "more favorably" for the same product-alternative product pair as the prohibited basis group. (Again refer to table B, in the sample size tables and marginal applicant processes noted above in selecting the sample.)

e. Compare the qualifications of the benchmark applicant with those of the control group applicants, beginning with the least qualified member of that sample. Any control group applicant who appears less qualified than the benchmark applicant should be identified on the spreadsheet as a "control group overlap."

f. Compare all control group overlaps with other less qualified prohibited basis group applicants to determine whether additional overlaps exist.

g. Document all overlaps as possible disparities in treatment. Discuss all overlaps and related findings (e.g., any differences between stated and actual underwriting criteria) with management, documenting all such conversations.

7. **Consult the supervisory office and, if appropriate, the Compliance Policy Division if you need to contact control group or prohibited basis group applicants to substantiate the steering analysis.**

NOTE: A bank violates ECOA, the FH Act, or both if, on a prohibited basis, it attempts to discourage or deter a credit seeker from applying at all (commonly called "pre-application screening"). There is some additional guidance on pre-application screening in section B of the "Other Types of Discrimination Analyses" (appendix G). However, pre-application screening on a prohibited basis cannot usually be detected through the types of analysis that can be conducted during an examination. If examiners find any indication that either steering or pre-application screening may be occurring, they should suggest the OCC consider pre-application testing of the bank.

Objective: Conduct Transactional Underwriting Analysis — Commercial Loans

Unlike consumer credit, when loan products and prices are generally homogenous and underwriting involves evaluating a limited number of credit variables, commercial loans are generally unique and underwriting methods and loan pricing may vary depending on a large number of credit variables. The additional credit analysis involved in underwriting commercial credit products will entail additional complexity in the sampling and discrimination analysis process. Although ECOA prohibits discrimination in all commercial credit activities of a covered bank, the agencies recognize that small businesses (sole proprietorships, partnerships, and small, closely-held corporations), including those operated by prohibited basis group members may have less experience in borrowing. Furthermore, small businesses may have fewer borrowing options, which may make them more vulnerable to discrimination. Therefore, in implementing these procedures, examinations should generally be focused on small business credit (commercial applicants that had gross revenues of $1,000,000 or less in the preceding fiscal year), absent some evidence that a focus on other commercial products would be more appropriate.

1. Understand Commercial Loan Policies

For the commercial product line selected for analysis, review credit policy guidelines and interview appropriate commercial loan managers and officers to obtain written and articulated standards used by the bank in evaluating commercial loan applications. Select or adapt questions from the "Underwriter Interview Guide" (appendix J) for the interviews.

2. Conduct Comparative File Review

a. Select all (or a maximum of 10) denied applications that were acted on during the three-month period prior to the examination. To the extent feasible, include denied applications from businesses that are (1) located in particular racial or national origin group and integrated geographies or (2) appear to be owned by prohibited basis group members, based on the names of the principals shown on applications or related documents. (In the case of banks that do a significant volume of commercial lending, review more than 10 applications.)

b. For each of the denied commercial applications selected, record specific information from loan files and through interviews with the appropriate loan officer(s), about the principal owners, the purpose of the loan, and the specific, pertinent financial information about the commercial enterprise, including type of business (retail, manufacturing, service, etc.), that was used by the bank to evaluate the credit request. Maintenance or use of data that identifies prohibited basis characteristics of those involved with the business (either in approved or denied loan applications) should be evaluated as a potential violation of Regulation B.

c. Select 10 approved loans that appear to be similar for business type, purpose of loan, loan amount, loan terms, and type of collateral, as the denied loans sampled. For example, if the denied loan sample includes applications for lines of credit to cover inventory purchases for retail businesses, select approved applications for lines of credit from retail businesses.

d. For each approved commercial loan application selected, obtain and record information parallel to that obtained for denied applications.

e. Compare the credit criteria considered in the credit process for each of the approved and denied applications to established underwriting standards, rather than comparing files directly.

f. Identify any deviations from credit standards for both approved and denied credit requests and differences in loan terms granted for approved credit requests.

---

g. Discuss with the commercial credit underwriter when deviations from credit standards and terms are noted, but are not explained in the file. Each discussion should be documented on an appropriate worksheet.

3. Conduct Targeted Sampling

a. If deviations from credit standards or pricing are not sufficiently explained by other factors either documented in the credit file or the commercial underwriter was not able to provide a reasonable explanation, determine if deviations were detrimental to any applicants of a particular prohibited basis group.

b. Consider employing the same techniques for determining race and gender characteristics of commercial applicants as those outlined in the consumer loan sampling procedures.

c. If members of one or more prohibited basis groups exist among commercial credit requests that were not underwritten according to established standards or received less favorable terms, select additional commercial loans. Select applicants that are members of the same prohibited basis group and select similarly situated control group credit requests in order to determine whether there is a pattern or practice of discrimination. Select these additional files based on the specific applicant circumstance(s) that appeared to have been viewed differently by lending personnel on a prohibited basis.

d. If there are not enough similarly situated applicants for comparison in the original sample period to draw a reasonable conclusion, expand the sample period. The expanded sample period should generally not go beyond the date of the prior examination.

Expanded Sampling Guidelines

a. Generally, the task of selecting an appropriate expanded sample of prohibited basis and control group applications for commercial loans will require examiner judgment. Select a sample that is large enough to draw a reasonable conclusion.

b. Select from the applications that were acted on during the initial sample period, but were not included in the initial sample, and select applications from prior time periods as necessary.

c. The expanded sample should include both approved and denied, prohibited basis and control group applications, when similar credit was requested by similar enterprises for similar purposes.

Objective: Determine Potential for Discriminatory "Redlining"

Traditional "redlining" is a form of illegal disparate treatment in which a bank provides unequal access to credit, or unequal terms of credit, because of the race, color, national origin, or other prohibited characteristic(s) of the residents of the area in which the credit seeker resides or will reside or in which the residential property to be mortgaged is located. The practice of targeting certain applicants or areas with less advantageous products or services based on prohibited characteristics may also constitute redlining.

The redlining analysis may be applied to determine whether, on a prohibited basis:

- A bank fails or refuses to extend credit in such an area;
- A bank targets certain borrowers or certain areas with less advantageous products;
- A bank makes loans in such an area but at a restricted level or upon less-favorable terms or conditions as compared with contrasting areas; or
- A bank omits or excludes such an area from efforts to market residential loans or solicit customers for residential credit.

This guidance focuses on possible discrimination based on race or national origin. The same analysis could be adapted to evaluate relative access to credit for areas of geographical concentration on other prohibited bases — for example, age.

NOTE: Neither the Equal Credit Opportunity Act (ECOA) nor the Fair Housing Act (FH Act) specifically uses the term "redlining." However, federal courts as well as agencies that have enforcement responsibilities for the FH Act have interpreted redlining as prohibiting a bank from having different marketing or lending practices for certain geographic areas, compared with others, when the purpose or effect of such differences would be to discriminate on a prohibited basis. Similarly, the ECOA would prohibit treating applicants for credit differently on the basis of differences in the racial or ethnic composition of their respective neighborhoods.

Like other forms of disparate treatment, redlining can be proven by overt or comparative evidence. If any written or oral policy or bank statement (see redlining risk factors R6,- R10) suggests that the bank links the racial or national origin character of an area with any aspect of access to or terms of credit, refer to the procedures on documenting and evaluating overt evidence of discrimination.

Overt evidence includes not only explicit statements, but also any geographical terms used by the bank that would, to a reasonable person familiar with the community in question, connote a specific racial or national origin character. For example, if the principal information conveyed by the phrase "north of 110th Street" is that the indicated area is principally occupied by Hispanics, then a policy of not making credit available "north of 110th Street" is overt evidence of potential redlining on the basis of national origin.

Overt evidence is relatively uncommon. Consequently, the redlining analysis usually will focus on comparative evidence (similar to analyses of possible disparate treatment of individual customers) in which the bank's treatment of areas with contrasting racial or national origin characters is compared.

When the scoping process indicates that a redlining analysis should be initiated, consult the supervisory office and, if appropriate, the Compliance Policy Division before completing the following steps of comparative analysis:

- Identify and delineate any areas within the bank's CRA assessment area and reasonably expected market area for residential products that have a racial or national origin group character;
- Determine whether any area identified in step 1 appears to be excluded, under-served, selectively excluded from marketing efforts, or otherwise less-favorably treated in any way by the bank;
- Identify and delineate any areas within the bank's CRA assessment area and reasonably expected market area for residential products that are of a particular racial or national origin group character and that the bank appears to treat more favorably;
- Identify the location of any racial or national origin group areas located just outside the bank's CRA assessment area(s) and reasonably expected market area for residential products that may have been purposely excluded by the bank.

- Obtain the bank's explanation for the potential difference in treatment between the areas and evaluate whether it is credible and reasonable; and
- Obtain and evaluate other information that may support or contradict interpreting identified disparities to be the result of intentional illegal discrimination.

These steps are discussed as follows.

Although the six steps listed are presented below as examination steps in the order given above, recognize that a different order may be preferable in any given examination. For example, the bank's explanation (step 5) for one of the policies or patterns in question may already be documented in the CRA materials reviewed (step 1) and the CRA examiners may already have verified it, which may be sufficient for the redlining analysis.

As another example, as part of the scoping process, examiners may have reviewed an analysis of the geographic distribution of the bank's loan originations with respect to the racial and national origin composition of census tracts within its CRA assessment or residential market area. Such analysis might have documented the existence of significant discrepancies between areas, by degree of a particular racial or national origin group concentration, in loans originated (risk factor R1), approval/denial rates (risk factor R2) and/or rates of denials because of insufficient collateral (risk factor R3). In such a situation in which the scoping process has produced a reliable factual record, examiners could begin with step 5 (obtaining an explanation) of the redlining analysis below.

In contrast, when the scoping process only yields partial or questionable information, or when the risk factors on which the redlining analysis is based are complaints or allegations against the bank, steps 1 - 4 must be addressed.

1. **Identify and delineate any areas within the bank's CRA assessment area and reasonably expected market area for residential products that are of a racial or national origin group character.**

   NOTE: The CRA assessment area can be convenient for redlining analysis because information about it is typically already in hand. However, the CRA assessment area may be too limited. The redlining analysis focuses on the bank's decisions about how much access to credit to provide to different geographical areas. The areas for which those decisions can best be compared are areas where the bank actually marketed and provided credit and where it could reasonably be expected to have marketed and provided credit. Some of those areas might be beyond or otherwise different from the CRA assessment area.

A redlining analysis is not appropriate for areas that can not be identified for their racial or national origin group character within the bank's CRA assessment area and reasonably expected market area for residential products, (If there is a substantial but dispersed minority population, potential disparate treatment can be evaluated by a routine comparative file review of applicants.)

This step may have been substantially completed during scoping, but unresolved matters may remain. For example, several community spokespersons may allege that the bank is redlining, but disagree in defining the area. In these situations:

a. Describe as precisely as possible why a specific area is recognized in the community (perceptions of residents, etc.) and is objectively identifiable (based on census or other data) as having a particular racial or national origin group character.

    •   The most obvious identifier is the predominant racial or national origin group residents of the area. Document the percentages of racial or national origin groups residing within the census tracts that make up the area. Analyzing racial and national origin group concentrations in quantities (such as 0 to < =25%, > 25% to < = 50%, > 50% to < =75% and > 75%) or based on majority concentration (0 to < =50%, and > 50%) may be helpful. However, remember that it is illegal for the bank to consider a prohibited factor in any way. For example, an area or neighborhood may only have a racial or national origin group population of 20%, but if the area's concentration appears related to lending practices, it would be appropriate to use that area's level of concentration in the analysis. Contacts with community groups can be helpful to learn whether such subtle features of racial or ethnic character exist within a particular neighborhood.

    •   Geographical groupings that are convenient for CRA may obscure racial patterns. For example, an underserved, low-income, predominantly minority neighborhood that lies within a larger low-income area that primarily consisted of non-minority neighborhoods may seem adequately served when the entire low-income area is analyzed as a unit. However, a pattern of under service to racial or national origin group areas might be revealed if the low-income minority neighborhood shared a border with an underserved, middle-income, minority area and those two minority areas were grouped together for purposes of analysis.

b. Describe how the racial or national origin character changes across the suspected redlining area's various boundaries.

c. Document or estimate the demand for credit within the racial or national origin area. This may include the applicable demographics of the area, including the percentage of homeowners, the median house value, median family income, or the number of small businesses, etc. Review the bank's non-originated loan applications from the suspected redlined areas and, if available, the aggregate bank data for loans originated and applications received from the suspected redlined areas. Community contacts may also be helpful in determining the demand for such credit. If the racial or national origin group area does not have a significant amount or demand for such credit, the area is not appropriate for a redlining analysis.

2. **Determine whether any racial or national origin group area identified in step 1 is excluded, underserved, selectively excluded from marketing efforts, or otherwise less-favorably treated in any way by the bank.**

Begin with the risk factors identified during the scoping process. The unfavorable treatment may have been substantially documented during scoping and only needs to be finished in this step. If not, this step verifies and measures the extent to which HMDA data show the racial or national origin group areas identified in step 1 to be underserved and how the bank's explicit policies treat them less favorably.

a. Review prior CRA lending test analyses to learn whether they have identified any excluded or otherwise underserved areas or other significant geographical disparities in the bank's lending. Determine whether any of those are the racial or national origin group areas identified in step 1.

b. Learn from the bank itself whether, as a matter of policy, it treats any separate or distinct geographical areas within its marketing or service area differently from other areas. This may have been done completely or partially during scoping analysis related to risk factors R5 - R9. The differences in treatment can be in marketing, products offered, branch operations (including the services provided and the hours of operation), appraisal practices, application processing, approval requirements, pricing, loan conditions, evaluation of collateral, or any other policy or practice materially related to access to credit. Determine whether any of those less-favored areas are the racial or national origin group areas identified in step 1.

c. Obtain from the bank: (1) its reasons for such differences in policy, (2) how the differences are implemented, and (3) any specific conditions that must exist in an area for it to receive the particular treatment (more favorable or less favorable) that the bank has indicated.

3. **Identify and delineate any areas within the bank's CRA assessment area and reasonably expected market area for residential products that have a particular racial or national origin character and that the bank appears to treat more favorably.**

    To the extent not already completed during scoping:

    a. Document the percentages of control and prohibited basis groups residing within the census tract(s) that comprise(s) a particular racial or national origin group area.

    b. Document the nature of the housing stock in the area.

    c. Describe, to the extent known, how the bank's practices, policies, or its rate of lending change from less favorable to more favorable as one leaves the particular racial or national origin group area at its various boundaries. (Be particularly attentive to instances in which the boundaries between favored and disfavored areas deviate from boundaries the bank would reasonably be expected to follow, such as political boundaries or transportation barriers.)

    d. Consider whether, within a large area that is composed predominantly of households of a particular racial or national origin group, there are enclaves that are predominantly of a different racial or national origin group or whether, along the area's borders, there are irregularities where the different racial or national origin group is predominant. As part of the overall comparison, determine whether credit access within those small areas of different racial or national groups differs from credit access in the larger racial or national origin group area.

4. **Identify the location of any racial or national origin group areas located just outside the bank's CRA assessment area(s) and reasonably expected market area for residential products, that may have been purposely excluded by the bank.**

    Review the analysis from prior CRA examinations of whether the assessment area(s) appears to have been influenced by prohibited factors. If there are racial or national origin group areas that the bank excluded from the assessment area(s) improperly, consider whether they ought to be included in the redlining analysis. Analyze the bank's reasonably expected market area in the same manner.

5. **Obtain the bank's explanation for the potential difference in treatment between the areas and evaluate whether it is credible and reasonable.**

    This step completes the comparative analysis by soliciting from the bank any additional information not yet considered that may demonstrate that a non-discriminatory explanation for the potential disparate treatment based on race or ethnicity does exist.

    For each matter that requires explanation, provide the bank full information about what differences appear to exist in how the bank treats areas with particular racial or national origin group characteristics, and how examiners reached their preliminary conclusions at this stage of the analysis.

    a. Evaluate whether the conditions identified by the bank in step 2 as justifying more favorable treatment pursuant to bank policy existed in racial or national origin group neighborhoods that did not receive the favorable treatment called for by bank policy. If there are racial or national origin group areas for which those conditions existed, ask the bank to explain why the areas were treated differently despite the similar conditions.

    b. Evaluate whether the conditions identified by the bank in step 2 as justifying less favorable treatment pursuant to bank policy existed in neighborhoods with particular racial or national origin characteristics that received favorable treatment nevertheless. If there are areas with particular racial or national origin group characteristics for which those conditions existed, ask the bank to explain why those areas were treated differently, despite the similar conditions.

c. Obtain explanations from the bank for any potential differences in treatment observed that were not called for by the bank's policies.

- If the bank's explanation cites any specific conditions in areas with particular racial or national origin group characteristics to justify more favorable treatment, determine whether the areas with particular racial or national origin group characteristics identified in step 1 satisfied those conditions. If there are areas with particular racial or national origin group characteristics for which those conditions existed, ask the bank to explain why the areas were treated differently despite the similar conditions.

- If the bank's explanation cites any specific conditions in areas with particular racial or national origin group characteristics to justify less favorable treatment, determine whether the non-minority area(s) had those conditions. If there are areas with particular racial or national origin characteristics for which those conditions existed, ask the bank to explain why those areas were treated differently, despite the similar conditions.

d. Evaluate the bank's responses by applying appropriate principles selected from appendix C, "Evaluating Bank Responses to Evidence of Disparate Treatment."

6. **Obtain and evaluate specific types of other information that may support or contradict a finding of redlining.**

As a legal matter, discriminatory intent can be inferred merely from the lack of a legitimate explanation for clearly less-favorable treatment of particular racial or national origin groups. That might be the situation after step 4.Nevertheless, if the bank's explanations do not adequately account for a documented difference in treatment, consider additional information that might support or contradict the interpretation that the difference in treatment constituted redlining.

a. **Comparative file review.** Review the results of a comparative file review conducted with the redlining examination; or, clarify the appearance of discriminatory redlining, by comparing denied applications from within the suspected redlined area with approved applications from the contrasting area:

- Learn whether there were any denials of fully qualified applicants from the suspected redlined area. If so, that may support the view that the bank wanted to avoid doing business in the area.

- Learn whether the file review identified instances of illegal disparate treatment against applicants of the same race or national origin as the suspected redlined area. If so, that may support the view that the bank was avoiding doing business with applicants of that group, such as the residents of the suspected redlined area. Learn whether any such identified victims applied for transactions in the suspected redlined area.

- If there are instances of either of the above, identify denied residents of other racial or national origin groups, if any, of the suspected redlined area and review their application files to learn whether they appear to have been treated in an irregular or less favorable way. If so, that may support the view that the character of the area rather than of the applicants themselves appears to have influenced the credit decisions.

- Review withdrawn and incomplete applications for the suspected redlined area, if those can readily be identified from the HMDA-LAR, and learn whether there are reliable indications that the bank discouraged those applicants from applying. If so, that may support the view that the bank was avoiding conducting business in the area and may constitute evidence of a violation of section 202.4(b) of Regulation B.

Conversely, if the comparisons of individual transactions show that the bank treated all racial and national origin group applicants within and outside the suspected redlined area similarly, that tends to contradict the conclusion that the bank avoided the areas because it had racial and national origin group residents.

b. **Interviews of third parties.** The perspectives of third parties are taken into account by reviewing available materials during scoping. Later in the examination, information from third parties may help determine whether the bank's potential differences in treatment of areas with particular racial or national origin characteristics constitutes redlining.

- Identify persons (such as housing or credit counselors, home improvement contractors, or real estate and mortgage brokers) who may have extensive experience dealing with credit applicants from the suspected redlined area.

- After obtaining appropriate authorization and guidance from your supervisory office and, if appropriate, the Compliance Policy Division, interview those persons to learn of their first-hand experiences related to:

  - Oral statements or written indications by a bank's representatives that loan applications from a suspected redlined area were discouraged;

  - Whether the bank treated applicants from the suspected redlined area as called for in its own procedures (as examiners understand them) and/or whether it treated them similarly to applicants from areas with other racial or national origin group characteristics (as the examiners are familiar with those transactions);

  - Any unusual delays or irregularities in loan processing for transactions in the suspected redlined area; and

  - Differences in the bank's pricing, loan conditions, property valuation practices, etc., in the suspected redlined area compared with contrasting areas.

Also, gather from the third parties the names of any consumers they described as having experienced the questionable behavior recounted by the third party and consider contacting those consumers after consultation with the Compliance Policy Division.

If third parties witnessed specific conduct by the bank that indicates the bank wanted to avoid business from the area or prohibited basis group in question, this would tend to support interpreting the difference in treatment as intended. Conversely, if third parties report proper treatment or positive actions toward such area or prohibited basis group, this would tend to contradict the view that the bank intended to discriminate.

The work papers should describe whether and why examiners believe this information from third parties is reliable.

c. **Marketing**. A clear exclusion of the suspected redlined area from the bank's marketing of residential loan products supports the view that the bank did not want to do business in the area. Marketing decisions are affirmative acts to include or exclude areas. Disparities in marketing between two areas may reveal that the bank prefers one to the other. If sufficiently stark and supported by other evidence, a difference in marketing to racially different areas could itself be treated as a redlining violation of the Fair Housing Act. Even below that level of difference, marketing patterns can support or contradict the view that disparities in lending practices were intentional. Consequently:

   - Review materials that show how the bank has marketed in the suspected redlined area and in areas with other racial or national origin group characteristics. Begin with available CRA materials and discuss the issues with CRA examiners, then review other materials, as appropriate. The materials may include, for example, the bank's guidance for the geographical distribution of pre-approved solicitations for credit cards or home equity lines of credit, advertisements in local media or business or telephone directories, business development calls to real estate brokers, and calls by telemarketers.

   - Even if differences in marketing practices are not violations themselves, consider whether they are part of a pattern of evidence leading toward the conclusion that the bank intended to deal with groups selectively on a prohibited basis.

d. **Peer performance.** Market share analysis and other comparisons to competitors are insufficient by themselves to prove that a bank engaged in illegal redlining. By the same token, a bank cannot justify its own failure to market or lend in an area by citing other banks' failures to lend or market there.

However, a bank's inactivity in an underserved area where its acknowledged competitors are active would tend to support the interpretation that it intends to avoid doing business in the area. Conversely, if it is as active as other lenders that would suggest that it intends to compete for, rather than avoid, business in the area. Consequently:

- Develop a list of the bank's competitors.
- Learn the level of lending in the suspected redlining area by competitors. Check any public evaluations of similarly situated competitors obtained by the CRA examiners as part of evaluating the performance context or obtain such evaluations independently.

  e. **Bank's record.** Request from the bank information about its overall record of serving or attempting to serve the racial or national origin groups with which the suspected redlined area is identified. The record may reveal intent to serve that group that tends to contradict the view that the bank intends to discriminate against the group.

7. **For any information that supports interpreting the situation as illegal discrimination, obtain and evaluate an explanation from the bank.**

   NOTE: If the bank's explanation is that the disparate results are the consequence of a specific, neutral policy or practice that the bank applies broadly, such as not making loans on homes below a certain value, review the guidance in appendix G, "Disproportionate Adverse Impact," and consult the supervisory office and, if appropriate, the Compliance Policy Division.

Objective: Determine Potential for Discriminatory Marketing Practices

When scoping identifies significant risk factors (M1-M7) related to marketing, consult the supervisory office and, if appropriate, the Compliance Policy Division about a possible marketing discrimination analysis. If the supervisory office agrees to proceed, collect information as follows:

1. **Identify the bank's marketing initiatives**

   a. **Pre-approved solicitations**

   - Determine whether the bank sends out pre-approved solicitations:
     - For home purchase loans.
     - For home improvement loans.
     - For refinance loans.
   - Determine how the bank selects recipients for such solicitations.
     - Learn from the bank its criteria for such selections.
     - Review any guidance or other information the bank provided credit reporting companies or other companies that supply such lists.

b. **Media Usage**

- Determine in which newspapers and broadcast media the bank advertises.
  - Identify any racial or national origin identity associated with those media.
  - Determine whether those media focus on geographical communities of a particular racial or national origin character.
- Learn the bank's strategies for geographic and demographic distribution of advertisements.
- Obtain and review copies of the bank's printed advertising and promotional materials.
- Determine what criteria the bank communicates to media about what is an attractive customer or an attractive area to cultivate business.
- Determine whether advertising and marketing are the same regardless of the racial or national origin character of the area.

c. **Self-produced promotional materials**

- Learn how the bank distributes its own promotional materials, both methods and geographical distribution.
- Learn what the bank regards as the target audience(s) for those materials.

d. **Realtors, brokers, contractors, and other intermediaries**

- Determine whether the bank solicits business from specific realtors, brokers, home improvement contractors, and other conduits.
  - Learn how the bank decides which intermediaries it will solicit.
  - Identify the parties contacted and determine the distribution between different racial and ethnic areas.
  - Obtain and review the types of information the bank distributes to intermediaries.
  - Determine how often the bank contacts intermediaries.
- Determine what criteria the bank communicates to intermediaries about the type of customers it seeks or the nature of the geographic areas in which it wishes to do business.

e. **Telemarketers or predictive dialer programs**

- Learn how the bank identifies which customers to contact, and whether the bank sets any parameters on how the list of consumers is compiled.

2. **Decide whether the bank's activities show a significantly lower level of marketing effort toward racial or national origin group areas or toward media or intermediaries that tend to reach racial or national origin group areas.**

3. **If there is any such disparity, document the bank's explanation for it.**

For additional guidance on marketing, refer to part C of appendix G "Other Types of Discrimination Analyses."

Objective: Consider the Effect of Credit Scoring

If the scoping process results in the selection of a focal point that includes a credit or mortgage scored loan product, refer to part C of the "Considering Automated Underwriting and Credit Scoring Risk Factors" (appendix B).

If the bank uses a credit scoring program that scores age for any loan product selected for review in the scoping stage, either as the sole underwriting determinant or only as a guide to making loan decisions, refer to part D of the "Considering Automated Underwriting and Credit Scoring Risk Factors" (appendix B).

Objective: Consider Disparate Impact Issues

These procedures have thus far focused primarily on examining comparative evidence for possible unlawful disparate treatment. Disparate impact has been described briefly in the introduction. Whenever examiners believe that a particular bank policy or practice appears to have a disparate impact on a prohibited basis, refer to part A of the "Other Types of Discrimination Analyses" (appendix G) or consult the supervisory office and, if appropriate, the Compliance Policy Division for further guidance.

Concluding the Examination

1. **Present to the bank's management for explanation:**

   a. Any overt evidence of disparate treatment on a prohibited basis.

   b. All instances of potential disparate treatment (e.g., overlaps) in either the underwriting of loans or in loan prices, terms, or conditions.

   c. All instances of potential disparate treatment in the form of discriminatory steering, redlining, or marketing policies or practices.

   d. All instances when a denied prohibited basis applicant was not afforded the same level of assistance or the same benefit of discretion as an approved control group applicant who was no better qualified with regard to the reason for denial.

   e. All instances when a prohibited basis applicant received conspicuously less favorable treatment by the bank than was customary from the bank or was required by the bank's policy.

   f. Any statistically significant average difference in either the frequency or amount of pricing disparities between control group and prohibited basis group applicants.

   g. Any evidence of neutral policies, procedures, or practices that appear to have a disparate effect on a prohibited basis.

2. **Explain that unless there are legitimate, nondiscriminatory explanations (or in the case of disparate impact, a compelling business justification) for each of the preliminary findings of discrimination identified in this part, the agency could conclude that the bank is in violation of the applicable fair lending laws.**

3. **Present to bank management any apparent violation (even isolated) from the "Other Illegal Limitations on Credit Checklist" (appendix K) that was not explained adequately by the bank's staff.**

4. Review the information on the completed "Technical Compliance Checklist" (appendix L). Consult the supervisory office and, if appropriate, the Compliance Policy Division to determine whether any violations represent a pattern or practice. If so, determine the violations' root cause(s), inform management of the violations, and obtain commitment(s) for corrective action. (Referral of these violations to DOJ is not mandated by ECOA.)

5. Document all responses that have been provided by the bank, not just its "best" or "final" response. Document each discussion with dates, names, titles, questions, responses, any information that supports or undercuts the bank's credibility and any other information that bears on the issues raised in the discussion(s).

6   Evaluate whether the responses are consistent with previous statements, information obtained from file review, documents, reasonable banking practices, and other sources, and satisfy common-sense standards of logic and credibility.

    a. Do not speculate or assume that the bank's decision-maker had specific intentions or considerations in mind when he or she took the actions being evaluated. Do not, for example, conclude that because you have noticed a legitimate, nondiscriminatory reason for a denial (such as an applicant's credit weakness) that no discrimination occurred unless it is clear that, at the time of the denial, the bank actually based the denial on that reason.

    b. Perform follow-up file reviews and comparative analyses, as necessary, to determine the accuracy and credibility of the bank's explanations.

    c. Refer to "Evaluating Bank Responses to Evidence of Disparate Treatment" (appendix C) for guidance as to common types of responses.

    d. Refer to the "Disproportionate Adverse Impact Violations" portion of the "Other Types of Discrimination Analyses" (appendix G) for guidance on evaluating the bank's responses to potential disparate impact.

7. If, after completing steps 1 through 6, above, you conclude that the bank has failed to demonstrate adequately that one or more apparent violations had a legitimate nondiscriminatory basis or were otherwise lawful, prepare

a documented list or discussion of violations, or a draft examination report, as prescribed by OCC policy.

8. Consult the supervisory office and, if appropriate, the Compliance Policy Division, regarding whether (a) any violations should be referred to the Departments of Justice or Housing and Urban Development and (b) the OCC should undertake enforcement action.

Appendix A: Compliance Management Analysis Checklist

This checklist used in conjunction with determining the reliability of the bank's compliance management process, pages 35 and 36 of the examination scope procedures, allows examiners to evaluate the bank's capacity to prevent, identify, and self-correct fair lending violations in connection with the products or issues selected for analysis. The checklist is not, however, intended to be an absolute test of a bank's compliance management program. Bank programs containing all or most of the features described in the list may nonetheless be flawed for other reasons; conversely, a compliance program which encompasses only a portion of the factors listed below may nonetheless adequately support a strong program under appropriate circumstances. In short, examiners must exercise their best judgment in using this list and in assessing the overall quality of a bank's efforts to ensure fair lending compliance.

Use the checklist as follows:

- Complete relevant portions of the checklist when compliance information about the focal point to be examined is received in response to the Request Letter.

- Use the checklist to structure an interview of the compliance officer and record information obtained about the compliance management process.

- For banks selected in the random sample of banks to receive fair lending examinations, complete the checklist for the focal point selected for the scope of the examination. If the checklist documents that there are sound compliance measures for that focal point, the risk level is lower. Reduce the number of files reviewed during the examination commensurate with the lower risk level by using sample sizes lower in the ranges in the sample size tables.

- For focal points at banks identified through the OCC's risk-based screening process, complete the checklist, but select the largest sample sizes within the ranges corresponding to the volumes of applications for the focal point, unless the Compliance Management Process conclusions resolve concerns about the specific indications of risk that caused the bank to be selected for examination.

A. Preventive Measures

Determine whether policies and procedures exist that tend to prevent illegal disparate treatment in the transactions to be examined. There is no legal or OCC requirement for banks to conduct the activities listed below. The absence of any of these policies and practices is never, by itself, a violation.

If the transactions within the proposed scope are covered by a listed preventive measure, check the box in the left column. Reduce the sample size of the planned comparative file review to the degree that the preventive measures cover transactions within the proposed scope. Document findings in sufficient detail to justify any resulting reduction of the file review sample.

Examiners are not required to learn whether preventive measures apply to specific products outside the proposed scope. However, if the information obtained shows that the self-compliance measure is a general practice of the bank, check the box in the right column in order to assist future examination planning.

1. Lending practices and standards:

    a. Principal policy issues:

        ☐ ☐ Are underwriting practices clear, objective, and generally consistent with industry standards?

        ☐ ☐ Is pricing within reasonably confined ranges with guidance linking variations to risk and/or cost factors?

        ☐ ☐ Does management monitor the nature and frequency of exceptions to its standards?

        ☐ ☐ Are denial reasons accurately and promptly communicated to unsuccessful applicants?

        ☐ ☐ Are there clear and objective standards for referring applicants to (i) subsidiaries, affiliates, or other lending channels within the bank, (ii) classifying applicants as "prime" or "subprime" borrowers, or (iii) deciding what kinds of alternative loan products should be offered or recommended to applicants?

        ☐ ☐ Are loan officers required to document any deviation from the rate sheet?

☐ ☐ Does management monitor consumer complaints alleging discrimination in loan pricing or underwriting?

NOTE: The items above are not compliance measures, but they are fundamental features of lending that tend to work against disparate treatment.

b. Do training, application-processing aids, and other guidance correctly and adequately describe:

☐ ☐ Prohibited bases under ECOA, Regulation B, and the FH Act?
☐ ☐ Other Regulation B substantive credit access requirements (e.g., spousal signatures, improper inquiries, protected income)?

c. Is it specifically communicated to employees that they must not, on a prohibited basis:

☐ ☐ Refuse to deal with individuals inquiring about credit?
☐ ☐ Discourage inquiries or applicants by delays, discourtesy, or other means?
☐ ☐ Provide different, incomplete, or misleading information about the availability of loans, application requirements, and processing and approval standards or procedures (including selectively informing applicants about certain loan products while failing to inform them of alternatives)?
☐ ☐ Encourage or more vigorously assist only certain inquirers or applicants?
☐ ☐ Refer credit seekers to other lenders, more costly loan products, or loan products with potentially onerous features?
☐ ☐ Refer credit seekers to nontraditional products (i.e., negative amortization, interest only, or payment option adjustable rate mortgages) when they could have qualified for traditional mortgages?
☐ ☐ Waive or grant exceptions to application procedures or credit standards?
☐ ☐ State a willingness to negotiate?
☐ ☐ Use different procedures or standards to evaluate applications?
☐ ☐ Use different procedures to obtain and evaluate appraisals?
☐ ☐ Provide certain applicants opportunities to correct or explain adverse or inadequate information, or to provide additional information?
☐ ☐ Accept alternative proofs of creditworthiness?
☐ ☐ Require co-signers?

☐ ☐ Offer or authorize loan modifications?
☐ ☐ Suggest or permit loan assumptions?
☐ ☐ Impose late charges, reinstatement fees, etc.?
☐ ☐ Initiate collection or foreclosure?

d. Has the bank taken specific initiatives to prevent the following practices:

☐ ☐ Basing credit decisions on assumptions derived from racial, gender, and other stereotypes, rather than facts?
☐ ☐ Seeking consumers from a particular racial, ethnic, or religious group, or of a particular gender, to the exclusion of other types of consumers, on the basis of how "comfortable" the employee may feel in dealing with those different from him/her?
☐ ☐ Limiting the exchange of credit-related information or the bank's efforts to qualify an applicant from a prohibited basis group?
☐ ☐ Drawing the bank's CRA assessment area to unreasonably exclude particular racial or national origin group areas?
☐ ☐ Targeting certain borrowers or areas with less advantageous products?

e. Does the bank have procedures to ensure that it does not:

☐ ☐ State racial or ethnic limitations in advertisements?
☐ ☐ Employ code words or use photos in advertisements that convey racial or ethnic limitations or preferences?
☐ ☐ Place advertisements that a reasonable person would regard as indicating specific prohibited basis group consumers are less desirable?
☐ ☐ Advertise only in media serving areas of the market that are comprised of a particular racial or ethnic group?
☐ ☐ Conduct other forms of marketing differently in areas of particular racial or national origin group characteristics of the market?
☐ ☐ Market through brokers known to serve only one racial or ethnic group in the market?
☐ ☐ Use a prohibited basis in any pre-screened solicitation for residential credit?
☐ ☐ Provide financial incentives for loan officers to place applicants in nontraditional products or higher-risk products?

2. Compliance Audit Function: Does the Bank Attempt to Detect Prohibited Disparate Treatment by Self-test or Self-evaluation?

NOTE: A self-test is any program, practice, or study that is designed and specifically used to assess the bank's compliance with the ECOA and the FH Act. It creates data or factual information that is not otherwise available and cannot be derived from loan, application, or other records related to credit transactions (12 CFR 202.15(b)(1) and 24 CFR 100.141). Regulation B at 12 CFR 202.15 and the FH Act at 24 CFR 100.140 cover self-tests and indicate that the report or results of a "self-test" is privileged and if such material is shared with the OCC, the privilege would be waived. However, Section 607 of the Financial Services Regulatory Relief Act of 2006 (12 USC 1828(x)) allows banks to share such privileged information with its federal regulatory agency during supervisory activities without waiving, destroying, or otherwise affecting that privilege as to third parties, such as private litigants.

A self-evaluation, while generally having the same purpose as a self-test, does not create any new data or factual information, but uses data readily available in loan or application files and other records used in credit transactions and, therefore, does not meet the self-test definition.

See appendix H, "Using Self-Tests and Self-Evaluations to Streamline the Examination" for more information about self-tests and self-evaluations.

The following items are intended to obtain information about the bank's approach to self-testing and self-evaluation. Complete the checklist below for each self-evaluation and self-test that the bank performed. Evaluating the results of self-evaluations and self-tests is described in appendix H, "Using Self-Tests and Self-Evaluations to Streamline the Examination."

Mark the box if the answer is "yes" for the transactions within the scope. Because the questions apply only to transactions within the scope of the examination, there is no second box to check.

   a. Are the transactions reviewed by an independent analyst who:

       ☐ Is directed to report objective results?
       ☐ Has an adequate level of expertise?
       ☐ Produces written conclusions?

b. Does the bank's approach for self-evaluations and self-tests call for:

- [ ] Attempting to explain major patterns shown in the HMDA data?
- [ ] Determining whether actual practices and standards differ from stated ones and basing the evaluation on the actual practices?
- [ ] Evaluating whether the reasons cited for denial are supported by facts relied on by the decision maker at the time of the decision?
- [ ] Comparing the treatment of prohibited basis group applicants to control group applicants?
- [ ] Obtaining explanations from decision makers for any unfavorable treatment of the prohibited basis group that departed from policy or customary practice?
- [ ] Covering significant decision points in the loan process where disparate treatment might occur, including:
    - [ ] The approve/deny decision?
    - [ ] Pricing?
    - [ ] Other terms and conditions?

- [ ] Covering at least as many transactions as examiners would independently by using the "Fair Lending Sample Size Tables" (appendix D) for a product with the application volumes of the product to be evaluated?
- [ ] Maintaining information concerning personal characteristics collected as part of a self-test separately from application or loan files?
- [ ] Analyzing the data timely?
- [ ] Taking appropriate and timely corrective action?

c. In the bank's plan for comparing the treatment of prohibited basis group applicants with that of control group applicants:

- [ ] Are control and prohibited basis groups based on a prohibited basis found in ECOA or the FH Act and defined clearly to isolate that prohibited basis for analysis?
- [ ] Are appropriate data to be obtained to document treatment of applicants and the relative qualifications vis-à-vis the requirement in question?
- [ ] Will the data to be obtained reflect data on which decisions were based, not later or irrelevant information?
- [ ] Will the denied applicants' qualifications related to the stated reason

for denial be compared with the corresponding qualifications for approved applicants?

☐ Are comparisons designed to identify instances in which prohibited basis group applicants were treated less favorably than control group applicants who were no better qualified?

☐ Is the evaluation designed to determine whether control and prohibited basis group applicants were treated differently in the processes by which the bank helped applicants overcome obstacles and by which their qualifications were enhanced?

☐ Will responses and explanations be sought for any apparent disparate treatment on a prohibited basis or other apparent violations of credit rights?

☐ Are reasons cited by credit decision makers to justify or explain instances of apparent disparate treatment to be verified?

d. For self-tests under ECOA that involved the collection of applicant personal characteristics, did the bank:

1. Develop a written plan that describes or identifies the:

☐ Specific purpose of the self-test?
☐ Methodology to be used?
☐ Geographic area(s) to be covered?
☐ Type(s) of credit transactions to be reviewed?
☐ Entity that will conduct the test and analyze the data?
☐ Timing of the test, including start and end dates or the duration of the self-test?
☐ Other related self-test data that is not privileged?

2. Disclose at the time applicant characteristic information is requested, that:

☐ The applicant will not be required to provide the information?
☐ The creditor is requesting the information to monitor its compliance with ECOA?
☐ Federal law prohibits the creditor from discriminating on the basis of this information or on the basis of an applicant's decision not to furnish the information?
☐ If applicable, certain information will be collected based on visual observation or surname if not provided by the applicant?

B. Corrective Measures

1. Determine whether the bank has provisions to take appropriate corrective action and provide adequate relief to victims for any violations in the transactions you plan to review.

- Who is to receive the results of a self-evaluation or self-test?
- What decision process is supposed to follow delivery of the information?
- Is feedback to be given to staff whose actions are reviewed?
- What types of corrective action may occur?
- Are consumers to be:
  - ☐ Offered credit if they were improperly denied?
  - ☐ Compensated for any damages, both out of pocket and compensatory?
  - ☐ Notified of their legal rights?

2. Other corrective action:

- ☐ Are bank policies or procedures that may have contributed to the discrimination to be corrected?
- ☐ Are employees involved to be trained and disciplined?
- ☐ Is the need for community outreach programs and changes in marketing strategy or loan products to better serve areas of a particular racial or national origin group of the bank's market to be considered?
- ☐ Are audit and oversight systems to be improved to ensure there is not a recurrence of any identified discrimination?

Appendix B: Considering Automated Underwriting and Credit Scoring Risk Factors

These procedures are designed to help examiners draw and support lending conclusions for banks using automated underwriting or credit scoring risk factors.

Background

Regulation B defines a "credit scoring system" as "a system that evaluates an applicant's creditworthiness mechanically based on key attributes of the applicant and aspects of the transaction, and that determines, alone or in conjunction with an evaluation of additional information about the applicant, whether the applicant is deemed creditworthy." The OCC also uses the terms "scoring models" and "scorecard" to describe a credit scoring system.

For the comparative analyses described here, learn how the score, underwriting policies and requirements for unscored factors, and human judgment influence the credit decision and interact in the bank's underwriting process.

In the planning phase of an examination, consider including economists from Compliance Risk Analysis Division (Compliance RAD) as consultants on the examination. Credit scoring models are statistical models. Compliance RAD economists can review a credit scoring model for potential disparate treatment or disparate impact. In addition, Compliance RAD economists can review scorecard development, monitoring, and validation materials to judge whether the scoring system meets the requirements in Regulation B that apply when age is scored (i.e., the requirements for empirically derived, demonstrably statistically sound systems).

Objective: Gain an Understanding of the Structure and Organization of the Scoring System

1. **For each customized credit scoring model for any product, or for any credit scoring model used in connection with a product held in portfolio, identify and obtain:**

a. The number and inter-relationship of each model or scorecard applied to a particular product;

b. The purposes for which each scorecard is employed (e.g., approval decision, set credit limits, set pricing, determine processing requirements, etc.);

c. The developer of each scorecard (e.g., in-house department, affiliate, independent vendor name), the development process, and description of the development population used;

d. The types of monitoring reports, including data integrity checks, generated (including front-end, back-end, account management and any disparate impact analyses), the frequency of generation, and recent copies of each;

e. All policies applicable to the use of credit scoring;

f. Training materials and programs on credit scoring for employees, agents, and brokers involved in any aspect of retail lending;

g. Any action taken to revalidate or re-calibrate any model or scorecard used during the examination period and the reason(s) why;

h. The process, criteria, and authority for overrides, how override decisions are documented, what reports are available on override activity; and the number of all high-side and low-side overrides for each type of override occurring during the examination period and any guidance given to employees on their ability to override;

i. All cutoffs used for each scorecard throughout the examination period and the reasons for the cutoffs and any change made during the examination period;

j. All variables scored by each product's scorecard(s) and the values that each variable may take (**NOTE:** The variables themselves are not proprietary information, although how they are weighted may be);

k. The method used to select for disclosure those adverse action reasons arising from application of the model or scorecard;

l. Steps an application goes through before and after scoring;

m. How, and by whom, applicant data are obtained and characterized before being entered for credit scoring;

n. Whether assistance can be given to help applicants improve their qualification data; and

o. Any other way that intervention by the bank can affect the applicant's score or the outcome.

2. **For each judgmental underwriting system that includes as an underwriting criterion a standard credit bureau or secondary market credit score identify:**

a. The vendor of each credit score and any vendor recommendation or guidance on the usage of the score relied upon by the bank;

b. The bank's basis for using the particular bureau or secondary market score and the cutoff standards for each product's underwriting system and the reasons for the cutoffs and any changes to the same during the examination period;

c. The number of exceptions or overrides made to the credit score component of the underwriting criteria and the basis for those exceptions or overrides, including any guidance given to employees on their ability to depart from credit score underwriting standards; and

d. Types of monitoring reports generated on the judgmental system or its credit scoring component (including front-end, back-end, differential processing and disparate impact analysis), the frequency of generation and recent copies of each.

NOTE: For fair lending analysis, examiners typically need not inquire into the activities of credit bureaus or the accuracy of scores the bureaus calculated from consumers' credit histories. If a bank's policy is that a credit bureau score at a certain level is supposed to have certain consequences, determine whether control group and prohibited basis applicants at those levels received the same consequences.

Objective: Determine Accuracy of Denial Reasons Based on Credit Scores Used in Adverse Action Notices

1. **Determine the methodology used to select the reasons why adverse action was taken on a credit application denied on the basis of the applicant's credit score.**

2. **Compare the methodology used in the examples cited in the Commentary to Regulation B and decide acceptability against that standard.**

3. **Identify any consumer requests for reconsideration of credit score denial reasons and review the action taken by management for consistency across applicant groups.**

4. **When a credit score is used to differentiate application processing, and an applicant is denied for failure to attain a judgmental underwriting standard that would not be applied if the applicant had received a better credit score (thereby being considered in a different — presumably less stringent —**

application processing group), ensure that the adverse action notice also discloses the bases on which the applicant failed to attain the credit score required for consideration in the less stringent processing group.

Objective: Consider Disparate Treatment in the Application of Credit Scoring Programs

Scoring systems should be examined for both types of evidence of disparate treatment — overt and comparative. For any instances of apparent disparate treatment, the bank may respond in the same ways as discussed in Evaluating Responses to "Evaluating Bank Responses to Evidence of Disparate Treatment" (appendix C). Evaluate the responses in the same manner.

Overt Evidence of Disparate Treatment

The only permissible consideration of a prohibited basis in a credit scoring system is provided in Regulation B, which permits banks to consider age, as long as:

- Persons over 62 are not treated less favorably than those under 62; and
- The scoring system is certified to be empirically derived and demonstrably and statistically sound (12 CFR 202.6 (b)(2)(ii)).

How to determine those two facts is further detailed in section D below.

Determine whether the system makes any other overt distinctions on a prohibited basis. For example, there would appear to be a violation if the scoring system assigns different credit limits depending on the marital status of the applicant(s) or uses a different cutoff score on a prohibited basis for applicants. The bank should know and disclose the factors included in any scoring system it uses in credit decisions. In that way, the bank and the OCC can be sure that no prohibited factors are scored and that age, when scored, is treated in conformity with Regulation B.

If there is overt evidence that applicants in a credit scoring system are treated less favorably, on a prohibited basis (other than age), ask the bank to respond in writing, and evaluate the response in the same way they would for any other overt evidence of disparate treatment.

Comparative Evidence of Disparate Treatment

If credit scores are the sole basis for granting credit, the fact that two applicants have different scores means they are not "similarly situated." There is no disparate treatment if the different results are commensurate with the difference in scores, if those applicants have otherwise been treated similarly. Comparative analysis may be appropriate to evaluate possible disparate treatment for pre-scoring and post-scoring underwriting activity. This can be done by judgmental interpretation or statistical inferences from a statistical model.

1. **Determine what controls and policies management has implemented to ensure that the bank's credit scoring models or credit score criteria are not applied in a discriminatory manner, in particular:**

   a. Review bank guidance for using the credit scoring system, handling overrides, and processing applicants and determine how well that guidance is understood by employees and monitored by management.

   b. Review bank policies that permit overrides or that provide for different processing or underwriting requirements based on geographic identifiers or borrower score ranges to assure that these policies do not treat prohibited basis group applicants differently than other similarly situated applicants.

   Other override policies and practices that indicate the existence of broad discretion that might be applied discriminatorily are:

   - Excessive overrides.
   - Judgmental elements or subjective reviews that could reverse the result called for by the score.
   - Multiple judgmental criteria for overrides without explicit weighting or guidance as to which of these is most important.
   - Numerous rules that could lead underwriters to reverse the result called for by the score.
   - Overlays of the scorecard and underwriting policies (for example, income and debt were scored variables but there is also a maximum debt-to-income (DTI) requirement).
   - Frequent use of "other," "miscellaneous," etc., as the reason for override.

2. **As called for in steps 3 and 4 below, focus on judgmental decisions to approve or deny applications, that is, "overrides" of the result indicated by the score. "High-side" overrides are denials that have scores higher than the cutoff. "Low-side" overrides are approvals that have scores lower than the cutoff.**

Prior to initiating steps 2 and 3, consult the supervisory office and, if appropriate, the Compliance Policy Division about developing a preliminary statistical analysis to show whether overrides were:

*   Used in similar proportions within the control and prohibited basis groups.
*   Applied consistently to control and prohibited basis group applications with similar characteristics.

If the overall pattern of overrides raises concerns, the OCC will determine whether to use a statistical model. The volume of overrides must equal at least 50 from each of the four "quadrants" of favorably or unfavorably treated control group and prohibited basis group applicants.

The role and complexity of human judgment in the underwriting process influence whether a statistical model is appropriate: A manual comparative file review probably is sufficient if the underwriters' use of the score and other data is governed by straightforward guidelines, and decisions are well documented. Examiners may be directed to review files to determine whether legitimate, nondiscriminatory reasons exist for any differences identified through the preliminary statistical analysis. A statistical model may be appropriate if the use of the score and other criteria by the underwriters are vague, complex, subjective, and/or poorly documented.

3. **Evaluate whether any of the bases for granting credit to control group applicants who are low-side overrides are applicable to any prohibited basis group denials whose credit score was equal to or greater than the lowest score among the low-side overrides. If such cases are identified, obtain and evaluate management's conclusion that such different treatment is not a fair lending violation.**

4. **Evaluate whether any of the bases for denying credit to any prohibited basis group applicants who are high-side overrides are applicable to any control**

group approvals whose credit score was equal to or less than the highest score among the prohibited basis high-side overrides. If such cases are identified, obtain and evaluate management's conclusion that such different treatment is not a fair lending violation.

5. If credit scores are used to segment applicants into groups that receive different processing or are required to meet additional underwriting requirements (e.g., tiered risk underwriting), perform a comparative file review or confirm the results and adequacy of management's comparative file review that evaluates whether all applicants within each group are treated equally.

6. Conduct pre-scoring comparative analysis. The analysis focuses on whether disparate treatment occurred in collecting, classifying, or documenting data before being entered for credit scoring, and whether assistance was given selectively to improve qualifications. This typically is conducted by manual file review and judgmental comparison. The scoring system's database may help to identify marginal applicants for such a comparison.

   - Select 50 denied applicants from the prohibited basis group that have scores marginally below the cutoff.
   - Select 50 approved applicants from the control group that have scores marginally above the cutoff.
   - Compare the two groups to determine whether qualifications were characterized and assistance was provided consistently.

   If the volume of applications is large, consult the supervisory office and, if appropriate, the Compliance Policy Division about assistance in selecting the sample.

Objective: Evaluate Disparate Impact and Credit Scoring Algorithms

Consult the supervisory office and, if appropriate, the Compliance Policy Division to assess potential disparate treatment issues relating to the credit scoring algorithms.

Objective: Evaluate Credit Scoring Systems that Include an Applicant's Age

Regulation B expressly requires initial validation and periodic revalidation of a credit scoring system that considers an applicant's age. There are two ways a credit scoring system can consider age: 1) the system can be split into different scorecards depending on the age of the applicant; and 2) age may be directly scored as a variable. Both features may be present in some systems. Regulation B requires credit scoring systems that use age to be empirically derived and demonstrably and statistically sound (EDDSS). This means that such systems must fulfill the requirements of section 202.2(p)(1)(i) - (iv).

Age-Split Scorecards: If a system is split into two cards only and one card covers a wide age range that encompasses elderly applicants (applicants aged 62 or older), the system is treated as considering, but not scoring, age. Typically, the younger scorecard in an age-split system is used for applicants under a specific age between 25 and 30. The scorecard de-emphasizes factors such as the number of trade lines and the length of employment, and increases the negative weight of any derogatory information on the credit report. Systems such as these do not raise the issue of assigning a negative factor or value to the age of an elderly applicant. However, if age is scored as a variable directly (whether or not the system is age-split), or if elderly applicants are included in a card with a narrow age range in an age-split system, the system is treated as scoring age.

Scorecards that Score Age: If a scorecard scores age directly, in addition to meeting the EDDSS requirement, the creditor must ensure that the age of an elderly applicant is not assigned a negative factor or value. (See the staff commentary at 12 CFR 202.2(p) and 202.6(b)(2)). A negative factor or value means using a factor, value, or weight that is less favorable than the creditor's experience warrants or is less favorable than the factor, value, or weight assigned to the most favored age group below the age of 62 (12 CFR 202.2(v)).

1. **Obtain documentation provided by the developer of the scoring system and consult the OCC's most recent guidance to determine empirical derivation and statistical soundness. The OCC has provided guidance to national banks on evaluating the soundness of credit scoring systems. (See OCC Bulletin 97-24, "Credit Scoring Models," May 20, 1997.)**

2. **Determine whether the bank has reviewed the performance of its credit scoring system periodically and whether the product scored has operated in a changing economic and customer environment. If so, it is even more important that the bank has performed a review. If the bank scores age, but has not conducted a review despite changes that call the predictive value of the system into question, consult the supervisory office and, if appropriate,**

the Compliance Policy Division.

If the scoring system does not use age as a factor and does not split scorecards by age, do not expect the bank to have reviewed the performance of the system or to have had it re-validated for fair lending compliance. (Remind the bank that it is prudent to review and re-validate the system so that it operates at optimal predictability, but that is not a fair lending issue.)

The OCC may evaluate the variables used in a validated credit scoring system to determine whether they have a disparate impact on any basis prohibited by the fair lending laws. However, the OCC will conclude that a variable is justified by business necessity and does not warrant further scrutiny if the variable is statistically related to loan performance and has an understandable relationship to an individual applicant's creditworthiness.

Appendix C: Evaluating Bank Responses to Evidence of Disparate Treatment

This appendix discusses a bank's possible responses to comparative evidence of disparate treatment and overt evidence of disparate treatment.

A. Bank Responses to Comparative Evidence of Disparate Treatment

The following are responses that a bank may offer — separately or in combination — in an attempt to explain that the appearance of illegal disparate treatment is misleading, and that no violation has occurred. The responses, if true, may rebut the appearance of disparate treatment. Evaluate the validity and credibility of the responses. Some of the types of responses include lists of responses of each type that examiners often encounter; the lists are examples only, and banks may offer explanations not on the lists.

1. The bank's personnel were unaware of the prohibited basis identity of the applicant(s).

    If the bank claims to have been unaware of the prohibited basis identity (e.g., race) of an applicant or neighborhood, ask the bank to show that the application in question was processed in such a way that the bank's staff, which made the decisions, could not have learned the prohibited basis identity of the applicant.

    If the product is one for which the bank maintains prohibited basis monitoring information, assume that all employees could have taken those facts into account. Assume the same when there was face-to-face contact between any employee and the consumer.

    If other facts exist about the application from which an ordinary person would have recognized the applicant's prohibited basis identity (for example, an easily recognizable surname such as an Hispanic one), assume that the bank's staff drew the same conclusions. If the racial character of a community is in question, ask the bank to provide persuasive evidence of what would prevent its staff from knowing the racial character of any community in its service area.

2. The difference in treatment was justified by differences in the applicants (i.e. applicants not "similarly situated").

Ask the bank to account for the difference in treatment by pointing out a specific difference between the applicants' qualifications, or some factor not captured in the application but that legitimately makes one applicant more or less attractive to the bank, or some nonprohibited factor related to the processing of their applications. The difference identified by the bank must be important enough to justify the difference in the treatment in question.

The factors commonly cited to show that applicants are not similarly situated fall into two groups: those that can be evaluated by how consistently they are handled in other transactions, and those that cannot.

a. Verifying "not similarly situated" explanations by consistency.

The appearance of disparate treatment remains if a factor cited by the bank to justify favorable treatment for a control group applicant also exists for an otherwise similar prohibited basis group applicant who was treated unfavorably. Similarly, the appearance of disparate treatment remains if a factor cited by the bank to justify unfavorable treatment for a prohibited basis group applicant also exists for a control group applicant that received favorable treatment. If this is not so, ask the bank to document that the factor cited in its explanation was used consistently for control group and prohibited basis group applicants.

Among the responses that should be evaluated this way are:

- **Customer relationship.** Ask the bank to document that a customer relationship was also sometimes considered to the benefit of prohibited basis group applicants and/or that its absence worked against control group customers.
- **Loan not saleable or insurable.** If file review is still in progress, be alert for loans approved despite the claimed fatal problem. At a minimum, ask the bank to produce the text of the secondary market or insurer's specific requirement.
- **Differences in standards or procedures between branches or underwriters.** Ask the bank to provide transactions documenting that each of the two branches or underwriters applied its standards or procedures consistently to both prohibited basis and control group applications it

processed, and that each served similar proportions of the prohibited basis group.

- **Differences in applying the same standard (differences in "strictness") between underwriters, branches, etc.** Ask the bank to provide transactions documenting that the stricter employee, branch, etc., was strict for both prohibited basis and control group applicants and that the other was lenient for both, and that each served similar proportions of the prohibited basis group. The best evidence of this would be prohibited basis group applicants who received favorable treatment from the lenient branch and control group applicants who received less favorable treatment from the "strict" branch.
- **Standards or procedures changed during review period.** Ask the bank to provide transactions documenting that during each period the standards were applied consistently to both prohibited basis and control group applicants.
- **Employee misunderstood standard or procedure.** Ask the bank to provide transactions documenting that the misunderstanding influenced both prohibited basis and control group applications. If such information is not available, find no violation if the misunderstanding is a reasonable mistake.

In all of those situations, the bank's best response would be to show that the treatment in question occurred for both groups in proportion to their representation among otherwise comparable applicants.

b. Evaluating "not similarly situated" explanations by other means.

If consistency cannot be evaluated, consider an explanation favorably even without examples of its consistent use if:

- The factor is documented to exist in (or be absent from) the transactions, as claimed by the bank;
- A prudent loan officer would consider the factor that is consistent with the bank's policies and procedures;
- File review found no evidence that the factor is applied selectively on a prohibited basis (in other words, the bank's explanation is "not inconsistent with available information"); and
- The bank's description of the transaction generally is consistent and reasonable.

Some factors that may be impossible to compare for consistency are:

- **Unusual underwriting standard.** Ask the bank to show that the standard is prudent. If it is prudent and is not inconsistent with other information, accept this explanation although no documentation demonstrating that it is used consistently exists.

- **"Close calls."** The bank may claim that underwriters' opposite decisions on similar applicants reflects legitimate discretion that examiners should not second guess. That is not an acceptable explanation for identical applicants with different results, but is acceptable when the applicants have differing strengths and weaknesses that different underwriters might reasonably weigh differently. However, do not accept the explanation if other files reveal that these "strengths" or "weaknesses" are counted or ignored selectively on a prohibited basis. If the number of "close calls" exceeds 30, contact the supervisory office and, if appropriate, the Compliance Policy Division about the potential to use statistical analysis to determine whether a pattern on a prohibited basis exists.

- **"Character loan."** Expect the bank to identify specific facts or a specific history that make the applicant who is treated favorably a better risk than those treated less favorably.

- **"Accommodation loan."** There are many legitimate reasons that may make a transaction appealing to a bank apart from the familiar qualifications demanded by the secondary market and insurers. For example, a consumer may be related to or referred by an important customer, be a celebrity who would bring prestige to the bank, be an employee of an important business customer, etc. Making a loan to an otherwise unqualified control group applicant with such attributes while denying a loan to an otherwise similar prohibited basis group applicant without those attributes is not illegal discrimination. However, be skeptical when the bank cites reasons for "accommodations" that an ordinary prudent loan officer would not value.

- **"Gut feeling."** Be skeptical when a bank justifies an approval or denial by a general perception or reaction to the consumer. Such a perception or reaction may be linked to a racial or other stereotype that legally must not influence credit decisions. Ask whether any specific event or fact generated the reaction. Often, the loan officer can cite something specific that made him or her confident or uncomfortable about the consumer. There is no discrimination if it is credible that the bank indeed considered such a factor and did not apply it selectively on a prohibited basis.

c. Follow up customer contacts

If the bank's explanation of the handling of a particular transaction is based on consumer traits, actions, or desires not evident from the file, consider obtaining supervisory office authorization to contact the consumer to verify the bank's description. Such contacts need not be limited to possible victims of discrimination, but can include control group applicants or other witnesses.

When authorized by the supervisory office in consultation with the Compliance Policy Division, examiners may contact bank customers to gather additional facts necessary to determine whether a violation exists or to verify an explanation that lacks documentation.

3. The different results stemmed from an inadvertent error.

   If the bank claims that an identified error such as a miscalculation or misunderstanding caused the favorable or unfavorable result in question, evaluate whether the facts support the assertion that such an event occurred.

   If the bank claims that an "unidentified error" caused the favorable or unfavorable result in question, expect the bank to provide evidence that discrimination is inconsistent with its demonstrated conduct and, therefore, that discrimination is the less logical interpretation of the result. Consider the context (as described below).

   Consider the context when evaluating isolated, ambiguous instances of apparent disparate treatment. They should find no violation when circumstances contradict the interpretation that the bank intended to treat applicants from the prohibited basis group less favorably. For example, discrimination is doubtful as the cause of an isolated, ambiguous lending decision or inconsistency when the bank clearly is receptive toward applicants from the prohibited basis group (as evidenced by, for example, frequent loans or aggressive advertising to the prohibited basis group) and has a record of training and other substantive efforts to comply with anti-discrimination laws.

4. The apparent disparate treatment on a prohibited basis is a misleading portion of a larger pattern of random inconsistencies.

   Ask the bank to provide evidence that the unfavorable treatment is not limited to the prohibited basis group and that the favorable treatment is not limited to the control group. Without such examples, do not accept a bank's unsupported claim that otherwise inexplicable differences in treatment are distributed randomly.

If the bank can document that similarly situated prohibited basis group applicants received the favorable treatment in question approximately as frequently and in comparable degree as the control group applicants, conclude there is no violation.

NOTE: Transactions are relevant to "random inconsistency" only if they are "similarly situated" to those apparently treated unequally.

In examinations in which the OCC has access to a bank's detailed, automated database (such as for many credit-scored products), contact the supervisory office and, if appropriate, the Compliance Policy Division during the planning of the examination about involving the OCC's statistical experts to address random inconsistency issues. (Because the OCC's statistical modeling approach incorporates control group denials and prohibited basis group approvals and control group approvals and prohibited basis group denials, possible "random inconsistency" already is considered in the model's analysis.)

Although a bank may succeed in demonstrating that its treatment of applicants is random, inform the bank that its inconsistent practices create the risk of future disparate treatment and raise concerns about the adequacy of its controls.

5. The differences in loan terms and conditions are the result of different borrower risks/costs.

   The same analyses described in the preceding sections with regard to decisions to approve or deny loans also apply to pricing differences. Risks and costs are legitimate considerations in setting prices and other terms and conditions of loan products. However, generalized reference by the bank to "cost factors" is insufficient to explain pricing differences.

   If the bank claims that specific borrowers received different terms or conditions because of cost or risk considerations, ask the bank to identify specific risk or cost differences between those borrowers.

   If the bank claims that specific borrowers received different terms or conditions because they were not similarly situated as negotiators, consider whether application records might provide relevant evidence. If the records are not helpful, consider seeking authorization to contact consumers to learn whether the bank, in fact, behaved comparably toward prohibited basis and control group consumers. The contacts would be to learn such information as the bank's opening quote of terms to the consumer and the progress of the negotiations.

NOTE: This situation may be appropriate for consulting the supervisory office and, if appropriate, the Compliance Policy Division about the use of pre-application, matched-pair testing to document the bank's treatment of potential applicants.

If the bank responds that an average price difference between the control and prohibited basis groups is based on cost or risk factors, ask it to identify specific risk or cost differences between individual control group applicants with the lowest rates and prohibited basis group applicants with the highest rates that are significant enough to justify the pricing differences between them. If the distinguishing factors cited by the bank are legitimate and verifiable, as described in the sections above, remove those applications from the average price calculation. If the average prices for the remaining control group and prohibited basis group members still differ more than minimally, consult the supervisory office and, if appropriate, the Compliance Policy Division about obtaining an analysis of whether the difference is statistically significant. Find a violation only if (1) evidence of disparate treatment of similarly situated borrowers exists or (2) a particular risk factor exists that meets all the criteria for a disproportionate adverse impact violation.

B. Bank Responses to Overt Evidence of Disparate Treatment

1. Descriptive references vs. lending considerations

   A reference to race, gender, etc., does not constitute a violation if it is merely descriptive — for example, "the applicant was young." In contrast, when the reference reveals that the prohibited factor influenced the bank's decisions and/or consumer behavior, treat the situation as an apparent violation to which the bank must respond.

2. Personal opinions vs. lending considerations

If an employee involved with credit availability states unfavorable views regarding a racial group, gender, etc., but does not explicitly relate those views to credit decisions, review that employee's credit decisions for possible disparate treatment of the prohibited basis group described unfavorably. If no instances of apparent disparate treatment exist, treat the employee's views as permissible private opinions. Inform the bank that such views create a risk of future violations.

3. Stereotypes related to credit decisions

An apparent violation may exist when a prohibited factor influences a credit decision through a stereotype related to creditworthiness, although the action based on the stereotype seems well-intended — for example, a loan denial because "a single woman could not maintain a large house." If the stereotyped beliefs are offered as "explanations" for unfavorable treatment, regard such unfavorable treatment as apparent illegal disparate treatment. If the stereotype is only a general observation unrelated to particular transactions, review that employee's credit decisions for possible disparate treatment of the prohibited basis group in question. Inform the bank that such views create a risk of future violations.

4. Indirect reference to a prohibited factor

If negative views related to creditworthiness are described in nonprohibited terms, consider whether the terms would be understood commonly as surrogates for prohibited terms. If so, treat the situation as if explicit prohibited basis terms were used. For example, a bank's statement that "It's too risky to lend north of 110th Street" might be reasonably interpreted as a refusal to lend because of race if that portion of the bank's lending area north of 110th Street were predominantly Black and the area south White.

5. Lawful use of a prohibited factor

a. Special-Purpose Credit Program (SPCP)

If a bank claims that its use of a prohibited factor is lawful because it is operating an SPCP, ask the bank to document that its program conforms to the requirements of Regulation B. An SPCP must be defined in a written plan that existed before the bank made any decisions on loan applications under the program. The written plan must:

- Demonstrate that the program will benefit persons who would otherwise be denied credit or receive credit on less favorable terms; and
- State the date that the program will be in effect or when it will be re-evaluated.

No provision of a SPCP should deprive people who are not part of the target group of rights or opportunities they otherwise would have. Qualified programs operating on an otherwise-prohibited basis will not be cited as a violation.

NOTE: Inform the bank of a caveat that an OCC finding stating that "...a program is a lawful SPCP" is not absolute security against legal challenge by private parties. Suggest that a bank concerned about legal challenge from other quarters use exclusions or limitations that are not prohibited by ECOA or the FH Act, such as "first-time home buyer."

b. Second review program

Second review programs are permissible if they do no more than ensure that lending standards are applied fairly and uniformly to all applicants. For example, it is permissible to review the proposed denial of applicants who are members of a prohibited basis group by comparing their applications to the approved applications of similarly qualified individuals who are in the control group to determine whether the applications were evaluated consistently.

Ask the bank to demonstrate that the program is a safety net that merely attempts to prevent discrimination, and does not involve underwriting terms or practices that are preferential on a prohibited basis.

Statements indicating that the mission of the program is to apply different standards or efforts on behalf of a particular racial or other group constitute overt evidence of disparate treatment. Similarly, an apparent violation exists if comparative analysis of applicants who are processed through the second review and those who are not discloses dual standards related to the prohibited basis.

c. Affirmative marketing/advertising program

Affirmative advertising and marketing efforts that do not involve application of different lending standards are permissible under both the ECOA and the FH Act. For example, special outreach to a community of a particular racial or national origin characteristic would be permissible. However, advertising and marketing that suggests, on a prohibited basis, that applications are not welcome may violate the FH Act, ECOA, or Regulation B's prohibitions against discouraging applicants.

Appendix D: Fair Lending Sample Size Tables

In banks selected as part of the OCC's random sample of banks to receive fair lending examinations, select a sample size within the appropriate range based on risk. For banks and focal points selected through the risk-based screening process, use the maximum sample size for the range unless the Compliance Management Review resolves concerns about the specific indications of risk that caused the bank to be selected for examination.

NOTE: Do not use these tables to evaluate focal points that involve credit scoring systems or the results of self-evaluations or of self-tests. Instead, see "Considering Automated Underwriting and Credit Scoring Risk Factors" (appendix B) and "Using Self-Tests and Self-Evaluations to Streamline the Examination" (appendix H). **Do not use these tables when conducting a pricing examination. See note #1 for sample sizes for pricing examinations.**

Table A: Underwriting (Accept/Deny) Comparisons

Sample 1 Prohibited Basis Group Denials				Sample 2 Control Group Approvals		
Number of Denials or Approvals	5- 50	51 - 150	> 150	20- 50	51 - 250	> 250
Minimum to review:	All	51	75	20	51	100
Maximum to review:	50	100	150	5x prohibited basis group sample (up to 50)	5x prohibited basis group sample (up to 125)	5 x prohibited basis group sample (up to 300)

Table B: Terms and Conditions Comparisons

Sample 1 Prohibited Basis Group Approvals				Sample 2 Control Group Approvals		
Number of Approvals	5 - 25	26 - 100	> 100	20 - 50	51 - 250	> 250
Minimum to review:	All	26	50	20	40	60
Maximum to review:	25	50	75	5x prohibited basis group sample (up to 50)	5x prohibited basis group sample (up to 75)	5 x prohibited basis group sample (up to 100)

See explanatory notes on the following pages.

Explanatory Notes to Sample Size Tables

1. When performing a pricing examination, conduct a full file review over a specific time range when the pricing criteria were constant. Do not just review loans that received a rate-spread, but all pricing decisions for the specific product being reviewed.

2. When performing both underwriting and terms and conditions comparisons (**NOTE:** OCC examinations typically should include only one of the comparisons), use the same control group approval sample for both tasks.

3. If there are fewer than five prohibited basis denials or 20 control group approvals, refer to "Sample Size" instructions in the procedures.

4. "Minimum" and "maximum" sample sizes: select a sample size between the minimum and maximum identified above. Base the size for the sample on the level of risk identified during scoping and the outcome of the compliance management system review. Once the sample size has been determined, select individual transactions judgmentally (refer to procedures). If the minimum number of approved files called for in a sample-size table exceeds the maximum (as calculated using the table), select the smaller number of files for the approved sample.

5. If two prohibited basis groups (e.g., Black and Native American) are being compared against one control group, select a control group that is five times greater than the larger prohibited basis group sample, up to the maximum.

6. If the bank's discrimination risk profile identifies significant discrepancies in withdrawal/incomplete activity between the control group and prohibited basis group, or if the number of marginal prohibited basis group files available for sampling is small, consider supplementing samples by applying the following rules:

   - If prohibited basis group withdrawals/incompletes occur after the applicant has received an offer of credit that includes pricing terms, this is a reporting error under Regulation C (the bank should have reported the application as approved but not accepted), and, therefore, these applications should be included as prohibited basis group approvals in a terms and conditions comparative file analysis.

- If prohibited basis group incompletes occur due to lack of an applicant response with respect to an item that would give rise to a denial reason, then include these incompletes as denials for that reason when conducting an underwriting comparative file analysis.

Whenever possible, select the sample from the 12-month period immediately preceding the examination, not from an earlier period. In addition, transactions or classes of transactions of particular interest may be identified to include in the sample. For banks and mortgage companies listed on the final fair lending screening lists each year, use the appropriate HMDA data as follows:

- For banks and mortgage companies listed on the final fair lending screens for Mortgage Lending Underwriting, Terms and Conditions, Rate-Spread Mortgages, and Fed Output Reports, use the HMDA data for the year used to develop the screening lists.

- For banks and mortgage companies listed on the final Redlining and Marketing screen, use the HMDA data and any other data useful for conducting a redlining and marketing analysis for the year used to develop the screening list.

- For banks on the Random Sample and Credit Card Banks final screens, use the most current data for the focal points identified.

For banks selected in the random sample of banks to be examined, set the sample size based on the estimated risk of discrimination. The more risk factors identified during examination scoping and the weaker the compliance management process, the larger the sample should be within the range.

If no HMDA-LAR for the product exists and the bank is not subject to the Fair Housing Home Loan Data System requirements, request that the bank estimate or count the numbers of racial and national origin group applications for home purchase, or refinance loans. Alternatively, examiners themselves may count them. (This is feasible because Regulation B requires monitoring information for home purchase and refinance applications.)

Note: Regardless of application volume or sample size, any clear instance of potential disparate treatment – even if the comparison consists of only two files – must be treated as an apparent violation.

Appendix E: Identifying Marginal Transactions

This guidance is intended to help examiners identify denied and approved applications that were not either clearly qualified or unqualified, i.e., marginal transactions.

Marginal Denials

Denied applications with any or all the following characteristics are "marginal." Such denials are compared to marginal approved applications. Marginal denied applications include those that:

- Were close to satisfying the requirement that the adverse action notice said was the reason for denial;
- Were denied by the bank's rigid interpretation of inconsequential processing requirements;
- Were denied quickly for a reason that normally would take a longer time for an underwriter to evaluate;
- Involved an unfavorable subjective evaluation of facts that another person might reasonably have interpreted more favorably (for example, whether late payments actually showed a "pattern," or whether an explanation for a break in employment was "credible");
- Resulted from the bank's failure to take reasonable steps to obtain necessary information;
- Received unfavorable treatment as the result of a departure from customary practices or stated policies. For example, if it is the bank's stated policy to request an explanation of derogatory credit information, a failure to do so for a prohibited basis applicant would be a departure from customary practices or stated policies even if the derogatory information seems to be egregious;
- Were similar to an approved control group applicant who received unusual consideration or service, but were not provided such consideration or service;
- Received unfavorable treatment (for example, were denied or given various conditions or more processing obstacles) but appeared fully to meet the bank's stated requirements for favorable treatment (for example, approval on the terms sought);

- Received unfavorable treatment related to a policy or practice that was vague, and/or the file lacked documentation on the applicant's qualifications related to the reason for denial or other factor;
- Met common secondary market or industry standards although failing to meet the bank's more rigid standards;
- Had a strength that a prudent loan officer might believe outweighed the weaknesses cited as the basis for denial;
- Had a history of previously meeting a monthly housing obligation equivalent to or higher than the proposed debt; or
- Were denied for an apparently "serious" deficiency that may have been overcome easily. For example, an applicant's total debt ratio of 50 percent may appear to exceed grossly the banks guideline of 36 percent, but this may be easily corrected if the application lists assets to pay off sufficient nonhousing debts to reduce the ratio to the guideline, or if the bank were to count excluded part-time earnings described in the application.

Marginal Approvals

Approved applications with any or all of the following characteristics are "marginal." Such approvals are compared to marginal denied applications. Marginal approvals include those:

- Of which qualifications satisfied the bank's stated standard, but very narrowly;
- That bypassed stated processing requirements (such as verifications or deadlines);
- For which stated creditworthiness requirements were relaxed or waived;
- That, if the bank's own standards were not clear, fell short of common secondary market or industry lending standards;
- That a prudent conservative loan officer might have denied;
- Of which qualifications were raised to a qualifying level by assistance, proposals, counteroffers, favorable characterizations or questionable qualifications, etc.; or
- That, in any way, received unusual service or consideration that facilitated obtaining the credit.

Appendix F: Potential Scoping Information

This appendix offers a full range of documentation and other information that might be useful in an examination. In that sense, it is a "menu" of resources to be considered and selected from, depending on the nature and scope of the examination being conducted. Any decision to select one or more particular items from this appendix for inclusion in a particular examination should, of course, include consideration of any burdens to the agency and bank in assembling and providing the selected item(s).

For examinations of banks identified through the OCC's risk-based screening process, the scope often will have been set as part of the screening process. The information request usually should be restricted to the focal point identified as part of the screening process. Be mindful that material already in hand can expedite scoping and reduce the amount of information requested.

A. Internal Agency Documents and Records

1. Previous examination reports and related work papers for the most recent compliance/CRA and safety and soundness examinations.

2. Demographic data for the bank's assessment areas/markets.

3. Customer Assistance Group complaint data.

B. Information from the Bank

Prior to beginning an examination, request the bank to provide the information outlined below. This request should be made far enough in advance of the on-site phase of the examination to facilitate compliance by the bank. In some banks, examiners may not be able to review certain parts of this information until the on-site examination. Generally, request only those items that correspond to the product(s) and time period(s) being examined.

1. **Bank's Compliance Program** (For examinations that will include analysis of the bank's compliance program.)

a. Organization charts identifying those persons who have lending responsibilities or compliance, HMDA or CRA responsibilities, together with job descriptions for each such position.

b. Lists of any pending litigation or administrative proceedings concerning fair lending matters.

c. Results of self-evaluations, copies of audit or compliance reviews of the bank's program for compliance with fair lending laws and regulations, including both internal and independent audits.

   Note: The request should advise the lender that Section 607 of the Financial Services Regulatory Relief Act of 2006 (12 USC 1828(x)) allows banks to share privileged information on self-tests with its federal regulatory agency during supervisory activities without waiving, destroying, or otherwise affecting that privilege for other third parties.

d. Complaint file.

e. Any written or printed statements describing the bank's fair lending policies and/or procedures.

f. Training materials related to fair lending issues including records of attendance.

g. Records detailing policy exceptions or overrides, exception reporting and monitoring processes.

h. Any major policy or institutional changes since the last supervisory cycle and policies covering counteroffers and assistance-provided applicants.

2. Lending Policies/Loan Volume

a. Internal underwriting guidelines and lending policies for all consumer and commercial loan products. If guidelines or policies differ by branch or other geographic location, request copies of each variation.

b. A description of any credit scoring system(s) in use now or during the exam period.

Inquire as to whether a vendor or in-house system is used; the date of the last verification; the factors relied on to construct any in-house system and, if applicable, any judgmental criteria used in conjunction with the scoring system.

c. Pricing policies for each loan product and for both direct and indirect loans.

The bank should be specifically asked whether its pricing policies for any loan products include the use of "overages." The request should also ask whether the bank offers any "subprime" loan products for B, C, or D risk level customers or otherwise uses any form of risk-based pricing. A similar inquiry should be made regarding the use of any cost-based pricing. If any of these three forms are or have been in use since the last exam, the bank should provide pricing policy and practice details for each affected product, including the criteria for differentiating between each risk or cost level and any policies regarding overages. Regarding indirect lending, the bank should be asked to provide any forms of agreement (including compensation) with brokers/dealers, together with a description of the roles that both the bank and the dealer/broker play in each stage of the lending process.

d. A description of each form of compensation plan for all lending personnel and managers.

The fair lending laws do not prescribe or prohibit particular compensation schemes. Consider whether the compensation scheme creates incentives for the originator or loan officer that might affect the consumer's access to credit or terms of credit. Evaluate whether a comparative analysis can be developed for such decisions.

e. Advertising copy for all loan products.

f. The most recent HMDA-LAR, including unreported data, if available. Information should be provided on diskette, CD, or DVD, if possible.

The integrity of the bank's HMDA-LAR data should be verified prior to the pre-examination analysis. Verification should take place approximately two to three months prior to the on-site phase of the examination.

g. Any existing loan registers for each non-HMDA loan product.

Request loan registers for the three-month period preceding the date of the examination, together with any available lists of declined loan applicants for the same period. Registers/lists should contain, to the extent available, the complete name and address of loan applicants and applicable loan terms, including loan amount, interest rate, fees, repayment schedule, and collateral codes.

Even though banks are not required to maintain, for fair lending purposes, registers of lending activity other than the HMDA-LAR, ask whether such records exist for the focal point selected. This additional information may help in selecting samples, time periods, etc.

h. A description of any application or loan-level databases maintained for each loan product, including a description of all data fields within the database or data that can be linked at the loan level.

i. Forms used in the application and credit evaluation process for each loan product.

At a minimum, this request should include all types of credit applications, forms requesting financial information, underwriter worksheets, any form used for the collection of monitoring information, and any quality-control or second-review forms or worksheets.

j. Lists of service providers.

Service providers may include: brokers, realtors, real estate developers, appraisers, underwriters, home improvement contractors, and private mortgage insurance companies. Request the full name and address and geographic area served by each provider. Also, request documentation as to any fair lending requirements imposed on, or commitments required of, any of the bank's service providers.

The guidance in "c" above with regard to indirect lenders also applies to these third parties.

k. Addresses of any Internet site(s)

Internet home pages or similar sites that a bank may install on the Internet may provide information concerning the availability of credit, or the means for obtaining it. All such information must comply with the anti-discrimination requirements of the fair lending laws. In view of the increasing capacity to conduct transactions on the Internet, review a bank's Internet sites to ensure that all of the information or procedures set forth therein are in compliance with any applicable provisions of the fair lending laws and regulations.

3. Community Information

a. Demographic information prepared or used by the bank.

b. Any fair lending complaints received through the OCC's Customer Assistance Group (CAG) or otherwise and bank responses thereto.

Appendix G: Other Types of Discrimination Analyses

These procedures are intended to assist examiners who encounter indications of disproportionate adverse impact, discriminatory pre-application screening, and possible discriminatory marketing.

A. Disproportionate Adverse Impact Violations

When examiners encounter possible disproportionate adverse impact, review the five conditions listed below. When all five conditions exist, consult the supervisory office and, if appropriate, the Compliance Policy Division to determine whether to present the situation to the bank and solicit an explanation of the bank's business justification for the policy or criterion that appears to cause the disproportionate adverse impact. Note that condition 5 can be satisfied by either of two alternatives.

The contacts between examiners and banks described in this section are information-gathering contacts within the context of the examination and are not intended to serve as the formal notices and opportunities for response that the OCC's enforcement process might provide.

Also, the five conditions are not intended as authoritative statements of the legal elements of a disproportionate adverse impact proof of discrimination; they are paraphrases intended to give practical guidance on situations that call for more scrutiny and on which additional information is relevant.

NOTE: If a policy or criterion causing a disproportionate adverse impact on a prohibited basis (condition 3) appears likely, consult the supervisory office and, if appropriate, the Compliance Policy Division. Consult these offices also, if the policy or criterion is obviously related to predicting creditworthiness and is used in a way that is commensurate with its relationship to creditworthiness or is obviously related to some other basic aspect of prudent lending, and no equally effective alternative for it appears to exist. Examples are reliance on credit reports or use of debt-to-income ratio in a way that appears consistent with industry standards and with a prudent evaluation of credit risk.

Conditions

1. A specific policy or criterion is involved.

The policy or criterion suspected of producing a disproportionate adverse impact on a prohibited basis should be clear enough that the nature of action to correct the situation can be determined.

NOTE: Gross HMDA denial or approval rate disparities are not appropriate for disproportionate adverse impact analysis because they typically cannot be attributed to a specific policy or criterion. Similarly, a bank's policies of allowing employees to exercise discretion and to negotiate terms or conditions of credit can better be described as the absence of policies or criteria than as a situation in which a policy or criterion generates a disproportionate adverse impact. Broad discretion and vague standards raise concerns about discrimination, but examiners should focus on possible disparate treatment.

2. The policy or criterion on its stated terms is neutral for prohibited bases.

3. The policy or criterion disproportionately affects applicants or borrowers of a prohibited basis group.

The difference between the rate at which prohibited basis group members are harmed or excluded by the policy or criterion and the rate for control group members must be large enough that it is unlikely that it could have occurred by chance. If a reason to suspect a significant disproportionate adverse impact may exist, consult the supervisory office and, if appropriate, district counsel, and the Compliance Policy Division.

4. There is a causal relationship between the policy or criterion and the adverse result.

The link between the policy or criterion and the harmful or exclusionary effect must not be speculative. It must be clear that changing or terminating the policy or criterion would reduce the disproportion in the adverse result.

5. **Either a or b:**

   a. The policy or criterion has no clear rationale, appears to exist merely for convenience or to avoid a minimal expense, is far removed from common sense, or standard industry underwriting considerations or lending practices.

The legal doctrine of disproportionate adverse impact provides that the policy or criterion that causes the impact must be justified by "business necessity" if the bank is to avoid a violation. There is very little authoritative legal interpretation of that term with regard to lending, but that should not prevent examiners from making the preliminary inquiries called for in these procedures. For example, the rationale generally is not clear for basing credit decisions on factors such as location of residence, income level (per se, rather than relative to debt), and accounts with a finance company. If prohibited basis group applicants were denied loans significantly more frequently than control group applicants because they failed a bank's minimum income requirement, it would appear that the first four conditions plus 5a existed. Therefore, consult the supervisory office and, if appropriate, the Compliance Policy Division about obtaining the bank's response, as described in the following section.

b. **Alternatively**, although a sound justification for the policy may exist, an equally effective alternative apparently exists as well for accomplishing the same objective with a smaller disproportionate adverse impact.

The law does not require a bank to abandon a policy or criterion that is clearly the most effective method of accomplishing a legitimate business objective. However, if an alternative that is approximately equally effective is available that would cause a less-severe adverse impact, the policy or criterion in question may constitute a violation.

At any stage of the analysis of possible disproportionate adverse impact, if such an alternative appears to exist, and the first four conditions exist, consult the supervisory office and, if appropriate, the Compliance Policy Division on how to evaluate whether the alternative would be equally effective and would cause a less-severe impact. If the conclusion is that it would, solicit a response from the bank, as described in the following section.

Obtaining the bank's response

If the first four conditions plus either 5a or 5b appear to exist, consult the supervisory office and, if appropriate, the Compliance Policy Division about whether and how to inform the bank of the situation, and solicit the bank's response. The communication with the bank may include:

- The specific neutral policy or criterion that appears to cause a disproportionate adverse impact.
- How examiners learned about the policy.
- How widely examiners understand it to be implemented.
- How strictly they understand it to be applied.
- The prohibited basis on which the impact occurs.
- The magnitude of the impact.
- The nature of the injury to consumers.
- The data from which the impact was computed.

The communication should request that the bank provide any information supporting the business justification for the policy and request that the bank describe any alternatives it considered before adopting the policy or criterion at issue.

Evaluating and following up on the response

The analyses of "business necessity" and "less discriminatory alternative" tend to converge because of the close relationship of the questions of what purpose the policy or criterion serves and whether it is the most effective means to accomplish that purpose.

Evaluate whether the bank's response persuasively contradicts the existence of the significant disparity or establishes a business justification. Consult the supervisory office and, if appropriate, district counsel, and the Compliance Policy Division.

B. Discriminatory Pre-application Screening

When examiners encounter possible discriminatory pre-application screening, obtain an explanation for any:

- Withdrawals by applicants in prohibited basis groups without documentation of consumer intent to withdraw;
- Denials of applicants in prohibited basis groups without any documentation of applicant qualifications; or
- On a prohibited basis, selectively quoting unfavorable terms (for example, high fees or down payment requirements) to prospective applicants, or

---

quoting unfavorable terms to all prospective applicants but waiving such terms for control group applicants. (Evidence of this might be found in withdrawn or incomplete files.)

- Delays between application and action dates on a prohibited basis.

If the bank cannot explain the situations, consider obtaining authorization to contact the consumers to verify the bank's description of the transactions. Information from the consumer may help determine whether a violation occurred.

In some instances, such as possible "prescreening" of applicants by bank personnel, the results of the procedures discussed so far, including interviews with consumers, may be inconclusive in determining whether a violation has occurred. In those cases, examiners should consult their supervisory office and, if appropriate, the Compliance Policy Division regarding the possible use of "testers" to pose as similarly situated applicants, differing only as to race or other applicable prohibited basis characteristic, to determine and compare how the bank treats them in the application process.

C. Possible Discriminatory Marketing

NOTE: See also the objective in the examination procedure, "Determine potential for discriminatory marketing practices."

When encountering possible discriminatory marketing:

1. Obtain full documentation of the nature and extent, together with management's explanation, of any:

   - Prohibited basis limitations stated in advertisements;
   - Code words or photos in advertisements that convey prohibited limitations; or
   - Advertising patterns or practices that a reasonable person would believe indicate prohibited basis consumers are less desirable or are only eligible for certain products.

2. Obtain full documentation as to the nature and extent, together with management's explanation, for any situation in which the bank, despite the availability of other options in the market:

- Advertises only in media serving areas of a particular racial or national origin group within its market;
- Markets through brokers or other agents that the bank knows, or could reasonably be expected to know, to serve only one racial or ethnic group in the market; or
- Uses mailing or other distribution lists or other marketing techniques for pre-screened or other offerings of residential loan products* that:
    - Explicitly exclude groups of prospective borrowers on a prohibited basis; or
    - Exclude geographies (e.g., census tracts, ZIP codes) within the bank's marketing area that have demonstrably higher percentages of residents of a particular racial or national origin group than does the remainder of the marketing area, but which have income and other credit-related characteristics similar to the geographies that were targeted for marketing.
- Offers different products to such geographies, especially if subprime products are marketed primarily to racial or ethnic minorities.

*NOTE: Pre-screened solicitation of potential applicants on a prohibited basis is covered by the FH Act. Consequently, analyses of this form of potential marketing discrimination should be limited to residential loan products subject to coverage under the FH Act.

3. Evaluate management's response particularly with regard to the credibility of any nondiscriminatory reasons offered as explanations for any of the foregoing practices. Refer to "Evaluating Bank Responses to Evidence of Disparate Treatment" (appendix C) for guidance.

Appendix H: Using Self-Tests and Self-Evaluations to Streamline the Examination

The OCC classifies "self-assessments" by banks to determine the level and effectiveness of their fair lending performance into two types: "self-evaluations" of the bank's actual transactions and "self-tests." The term "self-evaluation" is not used in the fair lending legislation, but the OCC uses it to mean all types of self-assessments that do not fall within the statutory definition of self-test.

Banks may find it advantageous to conduct self-tests or self-evaluations to measure or monitor their compliance with ECOA and Regulation B. A self-test is any program, practice, or study that is designed and specifically used to assess the bank's compliance with fair lending laws, provided the self-test creates data not available or derived from loan, application or other records related to credit transactions (12 CFR 202.15(b)(1) and 24 CFR 100.140-100.148). For example, using testers to determine whether there is disparate treatment in the pre-application stage of credit shopping may constitute a self-test. A self-evaluation, while generally having the same purpose as a self-test, is not a self-test because it does not create any new data or factual information. Instead, it uses data readily available in loan or application files and other records used in credit transactions.

If the bank has performed any self-evaluations or self-tests, and examiners can confirm the reliability and appropriateness of the self-evaluations or the self-tests (or even parts of them), examiners need not repeat those tasks that the bank has performed appropriately.

NOTE: When the term self-evaluation is used below it is meant to include self-tests.

If a bank has performed a self-evaluation of any of the products selected for examination, obtain a copy thereof and follow the remaining procedures in this section.

Determine whether the research and analysis of the planned examination would duplicate the bank's own efforts. If the answers to questions A and B below are both "yes", each successive "yes" answer to questions C through L indicates that the bank's work up to that point can serve as a basis for eliminating steps for the examiners.

If the answer to either question A or B is "no", the self-evaluation cannot serve as a basis for eliminating examination steps. However, examiners should still use the remaining questions to assess the self-evaluation and communicate the findings to the bank so that it can improve its self-evaluation process.

A. Did the transactions covered by the self-evaluation occur not longer ago than two years prior to the examination? If the self-evaluation covered more than two years prior to the examination, incorporate only results from transactions in the most recent two years.

B. Did it cover the same product, prohibited basis, decision center, and stage of the lending process (for example, underwriting, setting of loan terms) as the planned examination?

C. Did the self-evaluation include comparative file review?

   NOTE: One type of "comparative file review" is statistical modeling to determine whether control group and prohibited basis group applicants were treated similarly. If a bank offers self-evaluation results based on a statistical model, consult the supervisory office and, if appropriate, the Compliance Policy Division about how to proceed.

D. Were control and prohibited basis groups defined accurately and consistently with ECOA and/or the FH Act?

To answer questions E, F, and G below, for the bank's control group sample and each of its prohibited basis group samples, request to review 10 percent (but not more than 50 for each group) of the transactions covered by the self-evaluation. For example, if the bank's self-evaluation reviewed 250 control group and 75 prohibited basis group transactions, plan to verify the data for 25 control group and seven prohibited basis group transactions.

E. Were the transactions selected for the self-evaluation chosen so as to focus on marginal applicants or, in the alternative, selected randomly?

F. Were the data analyzed (whether abstracted from files or obtained from electronic databases) accurate? Were those data actually relied on by the credit decision makers at the time of the decisions?

G. Did the 10 percent sample reviewed for question F also show that customer assistance and bank judgment that assisted or enabled applicants to qualify were recorded systematically and accurately and were compared for differences on any prohibited bases?

H. Were prohibited basis group applicants' qualifications related to the underwriting factor in question compared to corresponding qualifications of control group approvals? Specifically, for self-evaluations of approve/deny decisions, were the denied applicants' qualifications related to the stated reason for denial compared to the corresponding qualifications for approved applicants?

I. Did the self-evaluation sample cover at least as many transactions at the initial stage of review as examiners would initially have reviewed using the sampling guidance in these procedures?

If the bank's samples are significantly smaller than those in the sampling guidance but its methodology otherwise is sound, review additional transactions until the numbers of reviewed control group and prohibited basis group transactions equal the minimums for the initial stage of review in the sampling guidance.

The sample size tables set the number of files that should be reviewed to separate transactions that are marginal from those that are not. Neither examiners nor the bank are expected to analyze in detail every file in the sample set from the tables. If examiners need to review additional transactions, they should follow the file review steps in these procedures; that is, a quick first review to select marginal transactions, identification of "benchmarks" and "overlaps" (encompassing both the bank's data and the supplemental data collected by the examiners), and abstracting of detailed data only from certain marginal files. If there were such instances, proceed to question J and evaluate how the bank handled them.

J. Did the self-evaluation identify instances in which prohibited basis group applicants were treated less favorably than control group applicants who were no better qualified?

If all the previous questions have been answered affirmatively, examiners should be able to tell from the bank's spread sheet or other work papers whether applicants appear to have been treated inconsistently with their qualifications and whether there are differences in treatment between control and prohibited basis group applicants. If there were no such instances of apparent disparate treatment, incorporate the findings of the self-evaluation into the examination findings and indicate that those findings are based on verified data from the bank's self-evaluation.

K. Were explanations solicited for such instances from the persons responsible for the decisions?

L. Were the reasons cited by credit decision makers to justify or explain instances of apparent disparate treatment supported by legitimate, persuasive facts, or reasoning?

If the questions above are answered Yes, incorporate the findings of the self-evaluation (whether supporting compliance or violations) into the examination findings. Indicate that those findings are based on verified data from the bank's self-evaluation. In addition, consult the supervisory office and, if appropriate, the Compliance Policy Division regarding whether to conduct corroborative file analyses in addition to those performed by the bank.

If not all of the questions in the section above are answered "yes", resume the examination procedures at the point that the bank's reliable work would not be duplicated. In other words, use the reliable portion of the self-evaluation and correspondingly reduce independent comparative file review. For example, if the bank conducted a comparative file review that compared applicants' qualifications without taking into account the reasons they were denied, use the qualification data abstracted by the bank (if accurate) with the proviso of constructing independent comparisons structured around the reasons for denial.

If a bank has self-evaluation results based on a statistical model, inform the supervisory office and confer with Compliance RAD. The OCC will assess the bank's self-evaluation and determine the reliability of the bank's statistical model.

E███ ███ ███

If the bank's self-evaluation identified apparent violations, attempt to verify whether they existed rather than relying on the bank's conclusions. If the violations are verified, document fully how the violations were identified and verified and prepare to forward the information to be considered for appropriate enforcement. The results of self-evaluations are not exempt from legal requirements that the OCC refer fair lending violations to DOJ and/or notify HUD. Confer with the supervisory office, district counsel and, if appropriate, the Compliance Policy Division in such cases.

Do not suggest corrective action to the bank or characterize its corrective actions to date as adequate or inadequate at this time. Rather document whether any bank corrective action alleviated the violations and particularly note whether the bank responded to any apparent violations it identified as called for in the "Policy Statement on Discrimination in Lending" (appendix O), question 6, including, but not limited to:

- Identifying customers whose applications may have been processed inappropriately, offering to extend credit to applicants who were improperly denied, compensating them for any damages (both out of pocket and compensatory), and notifying them of their legal rights.

- Correcting any bank policies or procedures that may have contributed to the discrimination.

- Identifying and training and/or disciplining the employees involved.

- Considering the need for community outreach programs and/or changes in marketing strategy or loan products to better serve segments of a particular racial or national origin group within the bank's market.

- Improving audit and oversight systems to ensure that the discrimination does not recur.

Consider whether the effectiveness of corrective action has been compromised by any bank delays in taking the corrective action.

Dear [bank]:

A review of your bank's compliance with the anti-discrimination requirements of the Fair Housing Act, the Equal Credit Opportunity Act, and Regulation B is scheduled to commence □ □ TE]. Examiners plan to focus on possible disparate treatment of applicants from different □ □ □ □ □ O□ N□T□ON□□ O□□ □N □ □O□□ □□□□ EN□E□□□□□ E□ O□ □□□ O□ OT□ E□□. We plan to review □□□□□□ □□□□□ □O□ □ETT□N□ O□ □O□N □□ TE□□TE□□ □□□ □N□ □ ON□□T□ON□ O□ □O□□□□E□E□ □N□N□ O□ □TEE□□N□ O□ □ □□□ET□N□□ for □□ E□□T□□O□ □ □T□ during the period from □ □ TE□ to □ □ TE□ at □□□N□ O□ □N□ E□□ □□T□N□ □ENTE□□.

This examination is being conducted under the authority of 12 USC 481. However, it also constitutes an investigation within the meaning of section 3413(h)(1)(A) of the Right to Financial Privacy Act (RFPA), 12 USC 3401, et seq. Therefore, in accordance with section 3403(b) of the RFPA, the undersigned hereby certifies that the OCC has complied with the RFPA. Section 3417(c) of the act provides that good faith reliance upon this certification relieves your bank and its employees and agents of any possible liability to the customer in connection with the disclosure of the requested information.

To ensure early, prompt, and clear communication on any fair lending matters that need explanation, please designate a bank representative to serve as the fair lending liaison.

Please provide to this office a copy of your fair lending risk assessment within one week after receiving this letter. Additionally, enclosed is a list of other materials that you should deliver to this office or have available for review at the bank. □□ □□□□ O□□□ TE: T□ E □□□□□□ O□ □□O□□E□ □N □E□□ON□E TO O□□ □□E□□O□ □□E □ E□T □□ EN□□O□E□ □T□ E□□□E□ T□□T □ E□E□ □E□T □O□ TO □ □□E □□□□□□□E TO □□E□E□ ON□□TE□□E □ □□□□□ □E □□□ □□□ □□□□ □□ □□□ □□□ □□□□□□□ □□□□□□□ □ □□□□□□ □ □□□□□□□ □□□□ □□ □□□□□□□□ □□□ □□□ □ □□□□□□□ □□□ □□□□□ □□□

We will ask you to explain any apparent inconsistencies in treatment of applicants from the groups compared and to explain any other apparent evidence of violations. In such situations, we will describe to you the sorts of information that would illustrate that the inconsistencies are not based on prohibited factors. Your bank is assumed to be in compliance with discrimination laws, unless evidence indicates otherwise.

Please inform us whether credit scoring was used to underwrite any of the transactions we plan to review. Also, please inform us of anything we may not be aware of that would make it inappropriate to compare certain transactions within the proposed scope of the examination to other transactions within the scope (such as a change in underwriting standards during the proposed review period).

We may be able to streamline the examination if your bank has conducted a self-evaluation or a self-test you conducted that included comparisons to detect prohibited differences in treatment of applications within the proposed scope of our examination. A "self-test" is any program, practice, or study that is designed and specifically used to assess the bank's compliance with fair lending laws, provided the procedure creates data not available or derived from loan, application or other records related to credit transactions. (Note: Regulation B at 12 CFR 202.15 and the FH Act at 24 CFR 100.140 cover self-tests and indicate that the report or results of a "self-test" is privileged and if such material is shared with the OCC, privilege is waived.. However, Section 607 of the Financial Services Regulatory Relief Act of 2006 (12 USC 1828(x)) allows banks to share such privileged information with its federal regulatory agency during supervisory activities without waiving, destroying, or otherwise affecting that privilege to other third parties such as private litigants.) A "self-evaluation" is an analysis you derived from loan or application files or other records related to credit transactions. Please provide to this office any self-evaluations you conducted during the period [_____ to _____]

Sincerely,

Name
Title

Bank Name: Examiner:
Exam Date: Product:

As necessary, ask follow-up questions until it is clear how requirements or procedures apply to the files to be examined and until the rationales for unusual policies are understood. Items in □□□ are apparent violations if not carried out as prescribed in Regulation B. Examiners may conduct a second interview to discuss inconsistencies found during file reviews.

If the bank's standards are unclear or if loan files lack data on applicants' qualifications:

- Ask what specific problems were the basis for the reasons for denying applicants cited on the notices of adverse action.
- Using specific approved applicants, ask how the bank determined that they differed from the denied applicants.
- Use file comments (if any) that characterize qualifications as "good," "adequate," "weak," etc., as points of reference.

GENERAL	
1. Obtain from the chief underwriter an overview of the underwriting procedures and standards. Review written policies, procedures, standards, etc.	
2. Do underwriting policies differ across the different loan products within the loan purpose categories of the focal points for this exam? If yes, how?	
3. Do underwriting policies differ by lien status, occupancy, property type, loan purpose, or documentation type?	
4. Does your bank apply different standards in any of the geographical areas within the proposed scope of the examination? If so, why?	
5. Does your bank apply different standards based on the size of the loan or the value of the property securing the loan requested?	
6. Does your bank apply different standards based on the amount of the applicant's income?	
7. Are there any factors we have not addressed that might make it inappropriate to compare some transactions within the proposed scope to others?	

8. Please provide all policy manuals and underwriting guidelines for the products included in the focal points for this examination.	
9. Were there any policy changes during the period under review? If yes, are there changes that would preclude combining the data for the entire time period (i.e., prevent comparison over the entire time period)? Please provide a summary of all policy changes.	
10. Are there any other reasons why any two applications in the focal point could not be compared?	
11. If the focal point covers home improvement loans, are home improvement loans underwritten differently from home equity loans?	
12. Are any of the 2nd lien Home Purchase or Refinance loans piggyback loans? If so, how are underwriting policies different if it is a piggyback loan vs. a stand-alone 2nd lien loan?	
13. What creditworthiness factors does the bank consider when making underwriting decisions for these products?	
14. How are creditworthiness factors used – for example, do you use ranges of values for the FICO score, or LTV and apply different underwriting policies based on tiers that applicants fall into? Or, do you use an absolute cutoff for values of the credit score, LTV, or DTI?	
15. Obtain any exception reports maintained on loans approved despite failing to meet requirements. Learn who approves exceptions.	
▯▯▯▯ ▯▯ ▯▯▯▯▯ ▯▯▯ ▯▯▯▯▯ ▯▯▯▯▯ ▯▯▯▯▯ ▯▯▯ ▯▯▯▯ ▯▯▯ ▯ ▯▯▯▯ ▯▯ ▯ ▯▯▯▯▯ ▯▯ ▯▯▯▯▯ ▯ ▯▯▯▯ ▯▯ ▯ ▯▯▯▯▯ ▯▯ ▯▯▯ ▯▯▯▯▯ ▯▯ ▯ ▯ ▯▯▯▯▯ ▯▯ ▯▯▯▯▯ ▯▯ ▯▯▯▯▯ ▯▯▯▯▯ ▯▯ ▯▯ ▯	
17. Find out if a credit-scoring system is used. If so, obtain information and follow guidance as called for in appendix B, "Considering Automated Underwriting and Credit Scoring Risk Factors."	
18. Obtain copies of any consumer guidance on the loan process (such as: how to develop a viable application).	
19. Obtain copies of any checklists, log sheets, or other loan-processing aids used by bank personnel.	
▯▯ N▯ ▯T▯ ▯ T▯ ▯E	
1. Could you explain the bank's organization in terms of prime, subprime or near-prime units; or subsidiaries? Are there any differences in underwriting/pricing across units/subsidiaries?	

2. Could you explain the bank's organization in terms of channels – wholesale, retail, Internet, correspondent banking, etc.? Are there any differences in underwriting/pricing across channels?	
3. What are the bank's primary markets or geographic areas of operation?	
4. Where are the service centers for each business unit and/or channel?	
5. Could you explain how an applicant gets channeled to a particular business unit?	
6. Could you explain the relationship the bank has with brokers? (Correspondent vs. broker lending) What kind of discretion do brokers have in underwriting/pricing?	
7. Please provide a list of the specific products and programs within the loan purpose category of the focal point for this examination?	
⬛⬛⬛⬛⬛ T⬛ON ⬛⬛ O⬛ E⬛⬛	
1. Could you walk us through the application process for each of the relevant products in each channel and/or business unit?	
2. Where are applications accepted? Who handles them?	
3. Which bank or subsidiary staff meets face-to-face with applicants?	
4. Which bank staff review or have access to the applications with completed monitoring information?	
⬛⬛⬛⬛⬛ ⬛ ⬛⬛⬛⬛⬛ ⬛ ⬛⬛⬛ ⬛⬛⬛⬛⬛ ⬛⬛⬛⬛⬛⬛ ⬛ ⬛⬛⬛⬛⬛ ⬛⬛⬛ ⬛ ⬛⬛⬛ ⬛ ⬛⬛⬛ ⬛⬛⬛⬛ ⬛⬛ ⬛⬛⬛ ⬛ ⬛⬛⬛⬛ ⬛⬛⬛⬛ ⬛⬛⬛⬛⬛ ⬛⬛ ⬛⬛	
⬛⬛⬛⬛⬛ ⬛⬛⬛⬛⬛ ⬛⬛⬛ ⬛⬛⬛ ⬛⬛⬛⬛ ⬛⬛⬛ ⬛⬛⬛ ⬛⬛⬛⬛ ⬛⬛⬛⬛ ⬛⬛⬛ ⬛⬛⬛	
7. If the product is covered by HMDA, when and how are data entered on the LAR?	
8. What applicant information verifications are obtained? When and how?	
9. What happens if there is a problem obtaining verifications or if they are inconsistent with the application data?	
10. Is the applicant asked if assistance or explanation is needed?	
11. Is there a "conditional approval" stage in the process?	
12. Do files document conditions and attempts to resolve them?	
13. How long are terms locked in by a written or oral agreement?	
14. Under what circumstances are lock-ins extended?	
⬛⬛⬛⬛ ⬛⬛ ⬛⬛⬛⬛⬛ ⬛⬛⬛⬛ ⬛⬛⬛⬛ ⬛⬛ ⬛ ⬛⬛⬛⬛⬛ ⬛ ⬛⬛⬛ ⬛⬛⬛⬛ ⬛⬛⬛⬛ ⬛⬛ ⬛⬛⬛⬛ ⬛⬛⬛ ⬛⬛	

16. Do you discuss with applicants all loan products they qualify for, or only the product requested by the applicants?	
17. What is the extent of automation in underwriting? i. How is the risk level of an applicant determined? ii. Are the products being analyzed here eligible for automated underwriting? iii. Do you use the Desktop Underwriter, Loan Prospector or some customized system? iv. If applications are auto-decisioned, would the loan officer only be involved to verify information? If information cannot be verified what is the next step? v. Who has discretion during the underwriting process? vi. What controls are in place to monitor this discretion? vii. What percent of applications are automatically "approved" or automatically "denied" – without additional manual review? viii. If there are no automatic approvals or denials, what percent of applications that are on the path to approval after risk level determination are eventually denied, and what percent of applications on the path to denial are eventually approved? ix. If there are no automatic approvals or denials, what is the nature of the manual review? Is it primarily verification of information? x. Are there second reviews for denials? Are there any second reviews for approvals? Please explain what factors are considered during these second reviews.	
18. Are there any other aspects to the application process that we should keep in mind during our analysis?	
19. If an applicant is denied a loan for the product he or she was applying for, does the lender make an effort to offer other loan products more suitable? Please explain this process.	
20. Which loans are sold in the secondary market? Are different underwriting guidelines used for these loans?	
21. Is there a certain time limit to receiving required documentation? After the time limit has elapsed would the application be denied automatically?	

22. Is there guidance given to the applicant when there is documentation outstanding? If the loan officer follows up with the borrower, how many contacts would be made?	
<div align="center">E T TO</div>	
1. Which credit report is used?	
2. When multiple credit scores are obtained, which score is used – lowest or middle?	
3. Do you use any custom score – own or vendor product? Could you describe the elements used if it is a custom score?	
4. Is the credit score of both primary applicant and co-applicant used in the credit decision? If yes, how?	
5. Review with the underwriter a copy of each type of credit report used. Obtain copies of any code sheets or other guidance on using the credit report(s).	
6. At what stage of the transaction is a credit report obtained?	
7. Does the bureau send a copy of the report (or abstract) to consumers? Obtain a copy of the transmittal letter.	
8. Do you look at details in the credit report – if so, for all or only marginal applicants? Could you give examples?	
9. Do you consider compensating factors if creditworthiness factors are not satisfactory? Can you provide some examples?	
10. Does the bank require that corrected information come from the bureau, or will it accept corrected information directly from the customer?	
11. What constitutes a sufficient credit history on which to make a decision?	
12. Is a minimum number of accounts reported required?	
13. Is a minimum length of reported credit history required?	
14. Has the bank made loans to persons who did not meet these standards?	
15. In such a case, what evidence of creditworthiness substituted for the bureau report?	

░░░░ ░░ ░░░░░ ░░ ░░░░ ░░░░░░ ░░░░░░ ░░░ ░░░ ░░ ░ ░░░ ░░ ░░░░ ░░░░ ░░░░░ ░░░ ░░░░░ ░░░ ░░░░░░░░ ░░ ░ ░░░░░░ ░░ ░░░░ ░░ ░░ ░░░░░ ░ ░░░░░░ ░░░ ░░░░	
20. What credit history deficiencies would cause denial?	
21. Does a mortgage payment defect negate otherwise good credit? Does a good mortgage payment record offset other credit defects?	
22. How far into the past is derogatory information relevant?	
23. Does it matter if the debt has been paid?	
24. Is minor derogatory information ignored? What kinds?	
25. Does the bank solicit explanations? In what circumstances? Obtain the form letter to the applicant, if one exists. If the mode of contact is by phone rather than letter, are these noted in the file?	
26. What constitutes a "good" explanation?	
27. Is the failure to disclose serious derogatory information on the application fatal?	
28. Is derogatory information associated with a medical problem in the applicant's household treated differently than other derogatory information?	
29. How does the bank view judgments, repossessions, and collections?	
30. Under what circumstances would the bank lend to a customer with a bankruptcy in his or her record?	
31. How does the bank view inquiries? Would the bank ever deny a loan solely on the basis of inquiries?	
░░ N░ ░ TO ░░O░E	
1. What items must be covered by funds for closing?	
2. How many months of cash reserves are needed?	
3. When are funds from undocumented sources acceptable?	
4. Are applicants with inadequate or marginal cash to close advised on how gift funds may be applied?	
5. Are grants acceptable as gifts? From what sources?	
6. How does the bank assure that applicants are advised uniformly regarding the use of grants?	
7. May family or household cash be pooled for closing?	

8. How are funds to close documented by the applicant?	
E ⬛ ⬛O⬛⬛ ENT⬛ N⬛ ⬛N⬛ O⬛ E	
1. How many years on the job are required for income to be deemed stable? How many years in the line of work?	
2. What length of gap or frequency of changes in employment is regarded as negative? Are explanations routinely requested for employment negatives?	
3. How is stable income defined?	
4. Do loan originators routinely ask for verifiable unstable sources of income, such as overtime and seasonal work?	
5. Is rent paid by household members counted as income?	
6. Do loan originators routinely ask about rent paid by household members?	
7. Is any or all nontaxable income to be "grossed up"?	
8. Are applicants routinely asked whether they expect their income to rise? What type of documentation is needed to establish a projected increase?	
9. How is part-time income handled?	
10. How is annuity, pension, or retirement income handled?	
11. How is income from alimony, child support, and separate maintenance handled? How is income from public assistance handled?	
PROJECTED HOUSING COSTS AND DEBTS	
1. What types of debts are included or excluded from ratio calculations?	
2. Are certain types of accounts viewed more negatively than others, for example, revolving debt?	
3. Under what circumstances would an applicant be advised to pay down debts?	
4. Would the bank specify which debts should be paid off?	
DEBT RATIOS	
1. What maximum housing debt and total debt ratios are used?	
2. What is the source or rationale for them?	
3. What would justify approving an application with a ratio higher than the requirement?	
4. Are applicants with qualifying ratios ever refused because of debt considerations?	
COLLATERAL/APPRAISALS	
1. Are applicants advised of their right to obtain	

a copy of the appraisal report on their property? Is a copy routinely provided? If the ☐H☐A Code☐ applies, are applicants provided a copy of the appraisal upon completion or at least three days before closing unless they waive the right?	
2. Does the bank employ its own appraisers? If the FHFA Code applies, does the bank take appropriate steps to prevent the improper influencing of such in-house appraisers and affiliated appraisers, appraisal company, or appraisal management companies?	
3. Review the guidance the bank provides appraisers, whether employed or independent.	
4. What rules govern adjustments to initial appraised values? If the FHFA Code applies, ensure any such adjustments are consistent with the appraiser independence safeguard standards.	
5. Who reviews appraisals? If the FHFA Code applies, does the bank quality control test a randomly selected 10 percent of appraisals?	
6. When is PMI required?	
7. What does the bank do if a PMI company refuses to insure the loan?	
8. On adverse action notices and HMDA-LAR "reasons for denial," does the bank report PMI denials as "denied for PMI," or does it merely repeat the substantive reason that the PMI company cited?	
9. Under what circumstances would a lender order a second appraisal?	
10. If the FHFA Code applies, does the bank prohibit reliance on appraisals completed by mortgage brokers or other third parties?	
11. What steps does the bank take to ensure appraiser independence and that the appraiser is not coerced or influenced?	
GUARANTORS, ETC.	
1. Under what circumstances would a guarantor materially increase an applicant's likelihood of approval (e.g., if the applicant had bad ratios, poor credit history)?	
2. Are applicants with such weak qualifications routinely told that a guarantor would increase the likelihood of approval?	
DENIALS	
1. Obtain a list of the reasons for denial and review it with the interviewee.	

---

[5] The FHFA Code will apply to all conventional, single-family loans originated on or after May 1, 2009, that are sold to the Federal National Mortgage Association (Fannie Mae) or the Federal Home Loan Mortgage Corporation (Freddie Mac).

2. How is the adverse action notice prepared? Review it with the interviewee.	
3. How does the bank document the timely provision of adverse action notices?	
4. Are all denied applicants given a second review? Describe the review process.	
FATAL FLAWS AND DEROGATORIES	
1. Are there any "fatal" values for factors that would result in an automatic decline? Is there any written guidance for the same?	
2. Would a bankruptcy in the last six months be fatal – if not, what would be a compensating factor? Are there any other fatal flaws – e.g., LTV >125 or DTI >100, etc.?	
3. What is the time frame considered for derogatory factors? Is the magnitude of delinquencies considered as well? (e.g., x number of 30-day delinquencies compared to y number of 90-day delinquencies?) Also, within the time frame considered, would newer derogatories get more weight than older ones (e.g., if the time frame for bankruptcies is six months, would a bankruptcy which is one month old get more weight than a five- month-old bankruptcy?)	
4. Are there any compensating factors that can make up for derogatory information – can you provide some examples?	
SECONDARY MARKET CONSIDERATIONS	
1. To whom does the bank principally sell loans?	
2. Arrange to have copies of the loan purchasers' guidance available during file review.	
3. In what ways are bank standards different from those loan purchasers require?	
4. What have been the lender's experiences in attempting to persuade loan purchasers to reconsider refusals to purchase?	
PORTFOLIO LENDING	
1. Does the bank lend for its own portfolio?	
2. How do the requirements for this differ from those for loans to be sold?	
3. Does the bank hold loans to "season" them until sale? What features would cause a loan to be handled this way?	
4. Does the bank purchase loans?	
EXCEPTIONS/OVERRIDES	
1. Are there any exceptions to the bank's stated requirements? Can you provide examples? When would they be made?	
2. Does the bank produce (for its management's use) an "exceptions" report that lists all residential loans made that do not meet the bank's stated requirements? Obtain any such report for the period being examined in the fair lending review.	

3. At what level in the bank can loans be approved that fail to meet requirements?	
4. Are there any overrides? Do you generate a report or list of overrides or flag them?	
5. Is there written guidance on exceptions and overrides? If so, please provide.	
6. Who authorizes exceptions and/or overrides?	
7. Is any special consideration given based on customer relationship with the bank? If so, please explain.	
COMPENSATING/OFFSETTING FACTORS	
1. Do strong qualifications in certain areas overcome an applicant's failure to meet requirements in others?	
2. Describe specific factors that operate to overcome particular deficiencies (e.g., projected income compensates for excessive total debt ratio)?	
3. Are compensating factors formal or informal? (Obtain any written guidance.)	
4. What constitutes a "good customer relationship?"	
LOAN TERMS AND CONDITIONS	
1. How are prices set? Is there a range?	
2. Why would prices differ? Which aspects of pricing are fixed and which are discretionary?	
3. How are loan terms set? Why would loan terms vary?	
4. How is the down payment set? Why would requirements vary?	
5. How are collateral requirements set? Why would requirements vary?	
6. How are escrow amounts set? Why would they vary?	
7. What fees are imposed for the product? Why would they vary?	
8. Please provide a copy of each of the rate sheets you use? If rates change often, a set of rate sheets for one or a small number of dates would be sufficient.	
9. Please provide all policy manuals and pricing guidelines for the products included in the focal points for this exam.	
10. Does pricing policy differ across the different loan products within the loan purpose categories identified in the focal points? If yes, how?	
11. Does pricing vary across channels and/or geography? If yes, how? Could you provide a list of all of the areas that have their own rate sheets?	
12. Were there any policy changes in pricing during the period under review? If yes, would	

these changes preclude combining the data for the time period covered by this exam? Also, please provide a summary of these changes.	
13. Were there any special promotions during the period under analysis? If yes, please explain.	
14. Could you walk us through the pricing process for each of the relevant products in each channel and/or business unit? How do brokers price loans? Do they have different rate sheets? Are any rate sheets broker-specific?	
15. What are the reasons why interest rates would be lower than or greater than what appears on the pricing sheets?	

16. Please expand on the <u>discretionary</u> reasons for price differences?
  i.   Can you provide some examples of these reasons?
  ii. How is pricing influenced by loan officers?
 iii. Is loan officer compensation tied to pricing? If so, please explain.
  iv. How is pricing influenced by brokers?
  v.   How are brokers compensated?
  vi. Are there caps for broker compensation?
 vii. Who else has discretion during the pricing process?
viii. What controls are in place to monitor discretion in pricing?
  ix. Explain to what degree potential loan customers are allowed to negotiate a better interest rate/loan fees. Are loan officers or brokers allowed to deviate from the pricing sheets? If yes, to what degree, what are the criteria considered, and how are the pricing exceptions/pricing discretion documented?	

17. What fees are charged? When and why would charged fees differ? Is there any discretion in charging fees?	
18. Are there maximum and minimum fees? Any exceptions?	
19. Do any fees vary by state due to state-specific laws?	
20. Which fees affect the APR?	
21. Are loan customers allowed to buy down the interest rates by paying more in discount points? If yes, explain the criteria and provide written guidance regarding this practice.	
22. How are origination points, discount points, and YSP determined? Are there caps on each or caps on totals?	
23. If any of the 2nd lien loans are piggyback loans, i. How are pricing policies different if a product is a piggyback loan vs. a stand-alone second lien loan?	

ii. How are pricing policies different if the corresponding first lien is held with another bank? iii. Are first and second lien loans as part of a combo loan priced independently?	
⬛ILE DOCU⬛ ENTATION	
1. How are contacts with the customer documented?	
2. How are in-bank conferences (or other face-to-face encounters) with the applicant documented?	
3. What work sheets should be found in the typical file?	
ELECTRONIC DATA	
1. Can automatic approvals and denials be identified in the electronic data? That is, are there identifiers for automated approvals and/or denials; or identifiers for the output from an automated system (such as DU/LP)?	
2. Can "document type" be identified in the electronic data?	
3. Is product name available in the electronic data?	
4. Are applicant names and addresses available in the electronic data?	
5. Can piggyback loans be identified in the electronic data? If yes, can one also identify if the 1st lien is from this bank or from another bank?	
6. Can individual brokers be identified in the data?	
7. Is there electronic information on any of the following: number of trade lines; number of 30- 60- 90-day "lates" and the time period in which those "lates" occurred; incidence of bankruptcy and/or foreclosure; combined loan to value; combined debt to income; years in job; years in occupation; loan term; identifier for whether applicant uses ACH; override codes; collateral value; customer relationship; employment type (salaried or self-employed); any measure of "stable income"; indicator for first-time home buyer?	
8. Is there electronic information on any additional pricing variables that can be incorporated into the dataset – overages; underages; broker fees; total broker compensation; YSP; any other points and fees; rate lock date or period (15-30-45-60 days, etc.)?	
9. Could you also provide explanations for the variables provided in the electronic dataset?	
10. If you update DTI, LTV, or other credit variables during the underwriting process, does the updated information appear in the data?	

Appendix — Other Illegal Limitations on Credit Checklist

This checklist can be used for reviewing audit work papers, evaluating bank policies, performing transaction testing, and training, as appropriate. Only complete those aspects of the checklist that specifically relate to the issue being reviewed, evaluated, or tested, and retain those completed sections in the work papers.

Review compliance with these Regulation B provisions in all fair lending examinations that include review of files, and may elect to do so as part of a regular, scheduled supervisory activity during the supervisory cycle. Review the checklist before comparative file review to ensure that they recognize the listed violations. As the file review proceeds, note any violations observed on one master checklist (not checklists for individual transactions). If the examination does not include a comparative review of files, use the checklist to review in detail 10 diverse files (approvals and denials, different products, etc.).

Obtain explanations for any apparent violations from the bank staff responsible for the transactions.

Some violations on the checklist are not stated in terms of a prohibited basis. They are violations simply if the bank treated applicants other than as prescribed. Nevertheless, determine also whether the violations occurred selectively on a prohibited basis.

NOTE Citations are to Regulation B, 12 CFR 202.1 et seq.

When reviewing audit or evaluating bank policies, a "No" answer indicates a possible exception/deficiency and should be explained in the work papers. When performing transaction testing, a "No" answer indicates a possible violation and should be explained in the work papers. If a line item is not applicable within the area you are reviewing, just indicate "NA."

Underline the applicable use: Audit   Bank Policies   Transaction Testing

Apparent Violation (if No)	Yes	No	Basis for Conclusion
Rules Concerning Evaluation of Applications			
1. To the extent that a credit evaluation system directly considers the age of an applicant, is it empirically derived, demonstrably and statistically sound? (202.6(b)(2)(ii), .2(p))			
2. In an empirically derived, demonstrably and statistically sound credit scoring system is the age of an elderly applicant (62 or older) not assigned a negative factor or value? (202.6(b)(2)(ii))			
3. In a judgmental system, is the applicant's age or income derived from public assistance considered only for the purpose of determining a pertinent element of creditworthiness? (202.6(b)(2)(iii))			
4. In any system for evaluating creditworthiness is the age of an applicant 62 or older considered only to favor him or her? (202.6(b)(2)(iv))			
5. When evaluating the applicant's creditworthiness, does the bank not consider aggregate statistics or assumptions relative to the likelihood of bearing or rearing children? (202.6(b)(3))			
6. Does the bank count (and not discount or exclude) income derived from part-time employment or a retirement benefit? (202.6(b)(5))			
7. If an applicant relies on income from alimony, child support, or separate maintenance payments in applying for credit, does the bank consider such payments as income when they are likely to be consistently made? (202.6(b)(5))			
8. To the extent it considers credit history, does the bank consider: a. The credit history, when available, of accounts designated as accounts that the applicant and the applicant's spouse are permitted to use or for which both are contractually liable? (202.6(b)(6)(i)) b. At the applicant's request, information from the applicant indicating that past credit performance does not accurately reflect the applicant's creditworthiness? (202.6(b)(6)(ii))			

Apparent Violation (if No)	Yes	No	Basis for Conclusion
c. At the applicant's request, any credit history in the name of the applicant's spouse or former spouse that the applicant can demonstrate accurately reflects the applicant's creditworthiness? (202.6(b)(6)(iii))			
9. Are married and unmarried applicants evaluated by the same standards? (202.6(b)(8))			
10. Are joint applicants treated in the same manner regardless of existence, absence, or likelihood of a marital relationship? (202.6(b)(8))			
Rules Concerning Extensions of Credit			
11. Does the bank allow an applicant to open or maintain an account in birth-given names or combinations of birth-given and married names, if requested? (202.7(b))			
12. Does the bank permit holders of open-end accounts to retain the accounts and not change the terms despite the account-holder's retiring, or changes in age, name, or marital status?(202.7(c)(1))			
13. If the bank requires reapplication for an open-end account based on a change in marital status of the applicant when the original credit decision was based, in whole or in part, on the income of the spouse; did the bank have information available indicating that the applicant's income may not support the amount of credit currently available? (202.7(c)(2))			
14. If jointly owned property is relied on to satisfy the standards of creditworthiness in the case of unsecured credit, are nonapplicant joint owners required to sign only instruments related to collateral?(202.7(d)(2))			
15. Is an applicant who qualifies individually allowed to obtain credit without a spouse's or other person's signature (other than as a joint applicant), or if an additional party is needed to support the credit requested, is the applicant allowed to request a person other than the spouse to serve as the additional party?(202.7(d) (1) and (5))			
16. Does the bank grant credit even if credit life, health, accident, or disability insurance is not available because of the applicant's age? (202.7(e))			

General Rule			
17. Do the bank's marketing or advertising materials contain any information that would discourage, on a prohibited basis, a reasonable person from making or pursuing an application?(202.4(b))			

Appendix L: Technical Compliance Checklist

This checklist can be used to review audit work papers, evaluate bank policies, perform transaction testing, and assess training as appropriate. Only complete those aspects of the checklist that specifically relate to the issue being reviewed, evaluated, or tested, and retain those completed sections in the work papers.

Review compliance with these Regulation B provisions in all fair lending examinations that include review of files, and, as appropriate do so as part of a regularly scheduled supervisory activity that includes a review of fair lending risk.

Use copies of this checklist to review in detail one approved and one denied consumer, business, and residential real estate file. If there appear to be any violations in those six files, maintain one master checklist during comparative file review (if there is one) to note any observed recurrence of the violations. If there are recurring violations, consult the supervisory office to determine whether any violations represent a pattern or practice. If so, the root causes must be determined, the violations must be presented to management, and commitments for corrective action must be obtained.

NOTE: Citations are to Regulation B, 12 CFR 202.1 et seq., unless indicated otherwise.

When reviewing audit or evaluating bank policies, a "No" answer indicates a possible exception/deficiency and should be explained in the work papers. When performing transaction testing, a "No" answer indicates a possible violation and should be explained in the work papers. If a line item is not applicable within the area you are reviewing, simply indicate "NA."

Underline the applicable use: Audit   Bank Policies   Transaction Testing

Apparent Violation (if No)	Yes	No	Basis for Conclusion
Information for Monitoring Purposes			
1. Do files for purchase and refinance loans for primary residences that are secured by the dwelling show that the bank requested monitoring information (202.13(a) and (b)) and that it noted this information on the application form or on a separate form referring to the application (202.13(b)): a. Ethnicity, using the categories "Hispanic or Latino," and "Not Hispanic or Latino"; and race, using the categories "American Indian or Alaska Native," "Asian," "Black or African American," "Native Hawaiian or Other Pacific Islander," and "White," and allowing applicants to select more than one racial designation (Comment 13(b)-1)? b. Sex? c. Marital status, using the categories married, unmarried, and separated? d. Age?			
2. Does the form used to collect monitoring information contain written notice that it is for federal government monitoring of compliance with federal statutes prohibiting discrimination on those bases, and that the bank must note ethnicity, race, and sex on the basis of sight and/or surname if the applicant chooses not to do so, or does the loan file indicate that the borrower was otherwise notified of this fact? (202.13(c))			
3. Does the bank note on the monitoring form applicant's refusals to disclose monitoring information? (202.13(b))			
4. a. If the bank takes applications in person (including by electronic media that allows the bank to see the applicant), and if the applicant refuses to provide the monitoring information, does the bank, to the extent possible on the basis of sight or surname, note on the form the ethnicity, race, and sex of each applicant? (202.13(b), Comment 13(b)-4) b. If the bank receives applications by mail, telephone, or electronic media and if it is not evident on the face of the application how it was received, does the bank indicate on the form or in the loan file how it was			

Apparent Violation (if No)	Yes	No	Basis for Conclusion
received?(Comments 13(b)-3, -4)?			
General Rules			
5. Are written applications used for home purchase and refinance transactions? (202.4(c))			
6. Are written disclosures clear, conspicuous and except for those required by 202.5 and 202.13, in a form the applicant can retain? (202.4(d)-1))			

7.
 	
  a. If disclosures are provided electronically, were they provided in compliance with consumer consent, i.e., the bank obtained the applicant's affirmative consent, and other applicable provisions of the E-Sign Act? (202.4(d)(2))
 	
  b. If disclosures required by 202.5(b)(1), 202.5(b)(2), 202.5(d)(1), 202.5(d)(2), 202.13, and 202.14(a)(2)(i) accompany an application that is accessed by the applicant in electronic form, were the required application-related disclosures provided in electronic form on or with the application form?			

Rules Concerning Requests for Information			
8. Do guidance and forms exclude requests for information relative to birth control practices, childbearing abilities, or childbearing or child-rearing intentions of the applicant, and does the loan file indicate that the bank did not otherwise inquire about these topics? (202.5(d)(3))			

9. Does the loan file indicate that the bank did not request information about spouses or former spouses except for transactions in which:
  a. The spouse will be permitted to use the account,
  b. The spouse will be contractually liable on the account,
  c. The applicant is relying on the spouse's income as a basis for repayment of the credit requested,
  d. The applicant resides in a community property state or is relying on property in such a state for repayment, or
  e. The applicant relies on alimony, child support, or separate maintenance payments from the spouse or the former spouse to repay the debt? (202.5(c))			

10. In the case of individual unsecured credit, does the loan file indicate that the bank made inquiries about the marital status of the			

Apparent Violation (if No)	Yes	No	Basis for Conclusion
applicant only when the applicant resides in a community property state or when community property is a basis for repayment of the debt, and do guidance and forms for unsecured individual loans include these inquiries? (202.5(d)(1))			
11. For loans other than individual unsecured credit, are inquiries into marital status no more extensive than obtaining the applicant's status as "married," "unmarried," or "separated"?(202.5(d)(1))			
12. If the loan file indicates that information was requested regarding whether income on the application is derived from alimony, child support, or separate maintenance payments, do guidance and forms ensure that the applicant is informed that such income need not be revealed if the applicant does not want the bank to consider the information in determining the applicant's creditworthiness? (202.5(d)(2))			
13. Is any special purpose program established and administered so as to avoid discriminating on a prohibited basis?(202.5(a)(3), 202.8)			
14. If the creditor collects information (in addition to required government monitoring information) on the race, color, religion, national origin, or sex of the applicant for purposes of a "self-test": a. Does the "self-test" meet the requirements of 202.15? b. Does the creditor disclose to the applicant, orally or in writing, when requesting the information that: i. The applicant is not required to provide information? ii. The bank is requesting information to monitor its compliance with ECOA? iii. Federal law prohibits the bank from discriminating on the basis of this information, or on the basis of an applicant's decision not to furnish the information? iv. If applicable, certain information will be collected based on visual observation or surname if not provided by the applicant or other person? (202.5(b))			
15. When a title, such as Ms., Miss, Mrs., or Mr., is requested on the application, does the form disclose that such designation is optional, and does the application form otherwise use			

Apparent Violation (if No)	Yes	No	Basis for Conclusion
only terms neutral as to sex? (202.5(b)(2))			
Rules Concerning Extensions of Credit			
16. For joint applications, do application files indicate an applicant's intent to apply for joint credit at the time of application? (202.7(d)(1)- 3)			
Notifications			
17. If the bank received more than 150 applications in the preceding year, do files show that the bank notified noncommercial applicants in writing of: a. Action taken, whether approval, counteroffer, or adverse action (within 30 days of receipt of a completed application), unless the application is approved and the parties contemplate that the applicant who has yet to inquire about the status of the application, will do so within 30 days after applying? (202.9(a)(1)(i), 202.9(e)) b. Adverse action because of incompleteness or a notice of missing information and that the information must be provided within a designated reasonable period for the application to be considered (within 30 days of receipt of the incomplete application)? (202.9(a)(1)(ii) and (c)(2)) c. Adverse action (within 30 days of taking such action) on existing accounts? (202.9(a)(1)(iii)) d. Adverse action (within 90 days after notifying the applicant of a counteroffer), if the applicant has not accepted the counteroffer (unless the notice of adverse action on the credit terms sought accompanied the counteroffer)? (202.9(a)(1)(iv))			
18. Do adverse action notices in denied files (as applicable) contain: a. A written statement of action taken and the name and address of the bank? (202.9(a)(2)) b. A written statement substantially similar to that in section 202.9(b)(1)? c. A written statement of specific reasons for the action taken or written disclosure as specified in 202.9(a)(2)(ii)) of the applicant's right to such a statement? (202.9(a)(2)(i) and (ii))			
19. In connection with credit other than an extension of trade credit, credit incident to a factoring agreement or other similar types of business credit, for businesses with revenues of $1 million or less in the preceding fiscal year, where the reasons were not given orally or in			

Apparent Violation (if No)	Yes	No	Basis for Conclusion
writing when adverse action was taken (under time frames in 202.9(a)(1)), was the disclosure of the right to a statement of reasons given in writing at the time of application in accordance with 202.9(a)(3)(i)(B)?			
20. For businesses with revenues in excess of $1 million in the preceding fiscal year, or for extensions of trade credit, credit incident to a factoring agreement or other similar types of business credit, was the notification of action taken communicated within a reasonable time orally or in writing, and were reasons for denial and the ECOA notice provided in writing in response to a written request for the reasons by the applicant within 60 days of the bank's notification? (202.9(a)(3)(ii)(B))			
21. Does the statement of reason(s) for adverse action contain the principal and specific reason(s) for the action?(202.9(b)(2))			
22. When an application involves multiple applicants, does the bank provide notification of action to the primary applicant, when one is readily apparent? (202.9(f))			
23. When an application is made to multiple creditors by a third party, and no credit is offered or extended by any of the creditors, does the bank ensure that the applicant is properly informed of the action taken? (202.9(g))			
Furnishing Credit Information			
24. If the bank furnishes information, a. Does the bank designate any new account to reflect the participation of both spouses if the applicant's spouse is permitted to use or is contractually liable on the account (other than as a guarantor, surety, endorser, or similar party) and any existing account within 90 days of the receipt of a request from one of the spouses for the designation? (202.10(a)) b. Does the bank furnish joint-account information to consumer reporting agencies in a manner that provides access to such information in the name of each spouse?(202.10(b))			
25. When the bank responds to an inquiry for credit information regarding a joint account, is the information furnished in the name of the spouse for whom the information is requested?(202.10(c))			

Record Retention			

26. Does the bank retain application files for 25 months (12 months for business credit applications from businesses with gross revenues of $1 million or less in the previous fiscal year, except an extension of trade credit, credit incident to a factoring agreement, or other similar types of business credit) after date of notice of action taken or notice of incompleteness the following (as applicable):
   a. The application and all supporting material? (202.12(b)(1)(i))
   b. All information obtained for monitoring purposes? (202.12(b)(1)(i))
   c. The notification of action taken, if written, or any notation or memorandum by the bank, if made orally? (202.12(b)(1)(ii)(A))
   d. A statement of specific reasons for adverse action, if written, or any notation or memorandum by the bank, if made orally? (202.12(b)(1)(ii)(B))
   e. Any written statement submitted by the applicant alleging a violation of ECOA or Regulation B? (202.12(b)(1)(iii))			

27. Does the bank retain application files in connection with existing accounts for 25 months (12 months for business credit applications from businesses with gross revenues of $1 million or less in the previous fiscal year, except an extension of trade credit, credit incident to a factoring agreement, or other similar types of business credit) after date of notice of action taken containing:
   a. Any written or recorded information concerning the adverse action? (202.12(b)(2)(i))
   b. Any written statement submitted by the applicant alleging a violation of ECOA or Regulation B?(202.12(b)(2)(ii))			

28. Does the bank retain application files for other applications for which section 202.9's notification requirements do not apply for 25 months (12 months for business credit applications from businesses with gross revenues of $1 million or less in the previous fiscal year, except an extension of trade credit, credit incident to a factoring agreement, or other similar types of business credit) after date the bank receives the application, containing all written or recorded information in its possession concerning the applicant, including any notation of action taken?(202.12(b)(3))			
29. For business credit applications from			

businesses with gross revenues of more than $1 million in the previous fiscal year, or an extension of trade credit, credit incident to a factoring agreement, or other similar types of business credit, does the bank retain records for at least 60 days after notifying the applicant of the action taken, or for 12 months after notifying the applicant of the action taken if the applicant requests within the 60-day time period the reasons for denial or that the records for the denial be retained?			

30. For prescreened solicitations, does the bank retain for 25 months (12 months for business credit except for businesses with gross revenues of more than $1 million in the previous fiscal year, or an extension of trade credit, credit incident to a factoring agreement, or other similar types of business credit) after the offer of credit was made:
  a. The text of any prescreened solicitation;
  b. The list of criteria the bank used to select potential recipients of the solicitation; and
  c. Any correspondence related to complaints (formal or informal) about the solicitation? (202.12(b)(7))			

31. If the bank has notice of an investigation, enforcement proceeding, or civil action under ECOA, was information subject to record retention requirements retained until final disposition of the matter? (202.12(b)(4))			

32. If the bank conducts a self-test pursuant to 202.15, does it, after completion of the test, retain all written and recorded information:
  a. For 25 months?
  b. Until final disposition if the self-test has actual notice that it is under investigation or subject to enforcement proceedings or a civil action? (202.12(b)(6))			

Rules on Providing Appraisal Reports			
33. Are applicants routinely given copies of appraisal reports used in connection with applications for credit secured by a lien on a dwelling, or are they provided with written notice (as specified in 202.14(a)(2)(i)), no later than when notified of the action taken under 202.9, of their right to obtain a copy of the appraisal report, and provided a copy of the appraisal report upon request in the manner specified in 202.14(a)(2)(ii)?			
Requirements for Electronic Communications			
Note The Federal Reserve Board has not yet			

mandated compliance with 202.16. Banks may follow 202.16 or their own policies as long as those policies comply with the requirements of the E-Sign Act, 15 USC 7001 et seq.			
34. If the bank uses electronic communication to provide any of the disclosures required by ECOA and Regulation B to be in writing, are the disclosures clear and conspicuous and in a form the applicant may retain? (202.16(b))			
35. If the bank uses electronic communications to provide disclosures that are required to be in writing (other than disclosures under 202.9(a)(3)(i)(B), 202.13(a), and 202.14(a)(2)(i), if provided on or with the application) does the bank obtain the applicant's affirmative consent? (202.16(c))			
36. If the bank uses electronic communication to provide disclosures, does the bank either a. Send the disclosures to the applicant's electronic address; or b. Make the disclosure available at another location and so notify the applicant by sending a notice that identifies the account involved and the address of the Internet Web site or other location where the disclosure is available, and make the disclosure available for at least 90 days after it is first available or after it sends the notice of the other location, whichever is later? (202.16(d))			
37. If a disclosure provided by electronic communication is returned, does the bank takes reasonable steps to attempt redelivery using information that is in its files? (202.16(e))			

Appendix M: Alternative Fair Lending Analyses

This appendix provides additional fair lending guidance for examining credit card banks (i.e., CEBA banks), high-volume credit card products at other national banks, and community banks that do not have enough lending activity to make comparative file review a meaningful examination strategy.

Credit Card Banks or Credit Card Departments of Banks

This guidance provides an alternative to comparative file review that should be more effective in evaluating and examining fair lending risk in credit card banks or banks with high-volume credit card products. Examiners should discuss these areas of concern with those banks as a part of ongoing bank supervision activities. Any questions about this advice or its implementation should be directed to the supervisory office and, if appropriate, the Compliance Policy Division.

Because of the difficulty in conducting comparative file reviews without government monitoring information, that form of analysis in credit card portfolios generally does not provide meaningful results. While the guidance in this appendix should be more appropriate in most instances, be prepared to conduct a comparative file review if they have information indicating that a bank is engaging in non-overt disparate treatment (i.e., treatment not based on formal written policy or practice) of applicants on a prohibited basis in its underwriting of applications or in the terms and conditions it offers to applicants.

Commence credit card examinations by obtaining information and reviewing each credit card product the bank offers to determine whether any are targeted toward a particular group on a prohibited basis. This information should include:

- The name of each product (e.g., bank card name, co-branded card names); information about what population each product is targeted to (e.g., current customers, customers applying at certain retail outlets);

- Copies of application forms for each product;

- The marketing plan and any solicitation and advertising materials used for each product;

- The terms and conditions for each product;

- The underwriting guidelines for each product (including pertinent credit scoring system documentation); and

- Different language credit card applications (e.g., Spanish language application). While offering different language applications is not illegal, banks should not offer different terms or apply different underwriting criteria to applicants based on whether they apply using a different language application.

Review how the bank markets its credit card products to different customer groups. Determine whether any marketing materials or the dissemination of those materials show on a prohibited basis a preference for any group of potential or actual customers.

Next, be alert for bank credit card programs that the bank states are special purpose credit programs or that are applied to specific prohibited basis groups, such as second review and lower interest rate cards, etc. For a program to qualify as a special purpose credit program, it must meet the guidelines delineated in Regulation B (Sec. 202.8). Banks that fail to follow those guidelines may be violating Regulation B even if their stated intention is to provide credit to underserved groups (e.g., blacks and Hispanics).

The issue of special purpose credit programs is complicated. Examiners who identify such programs should contact their compliance lead expert and, if appropriate, the Compliance Policy Division and the Community and Consumer Law Division for guidance. However, examiners should know that Regulation B does not allow banks to designate retroactively a program that treats applicants differently on a prohibited basis as a special purpose credit program.

Lastly, review all of the variables that go into each credit scorecard that the bank uses for any prohibited bases. Be especially careful to ensure that some less routinely discussed prohibited bases are not used as variables. An example of this would be a bank treating applicants who receive public assistance income less favorably by assigning them fewer points than applicants who receive the same amount of income from wages.

Along with reviewing credit scoring system variables, look at peripheral systems that feed application information into the credit scoring systems (e.g., automated application system). Ascertain whether the bank separates or tags applicants on a prohibited basis in a manner that causes them to be processed differently by a particular scorecard (e.g., assigning them different cut-off scores or lower credit line assignments) or to be processed in a way that causes applications to be evaluated by a completely different and less favorable scorecard.

The following examples illustrate how banks might employ policies that could violate Regulation B, based on marital status:

- A bank initiates an apparent difference in treatment in its credit scoring system by characterizing joint applicants as either "wedded" or "individual" in its automated application system. Thus, it prompts its credit scoring system to treat applicants differently based on whether they were married or unmarried joint applicants.

- A bank offers "honeymoon accounts," whereby it gives all applicants for that credit product $1000 lines of credit, regardless of whether they have any credit history or a credit bureau score. The bank denies persons who do not apply under this program if they do not have a credit history or credit bureau score.

- A bank does not allow "unmarried, joint applicants" for credit cards but does allow "married, joint applicants."

For additional information related to credit scoring systems, refer to Appendix B, "Considering Automated Underwriting and Credit Scoring Risk Factors."

Compliance with Substantive Provisions of Regulation B

This guidance covers situations in which the standard fair lending examination approach described in this booklet cannot be carried out or is not likely to yield meaningful results. Examiners should consult the supervisory office and, if appropriate, the Compliance Policy Division about the appropriateness of replacing the customary comparative file review with an analysis of the bank's compliance with certain substantive consumer

---

protections in Regulation B. As described below, these approaches either focus on prohibitive bases other than race or national origin or use an adaptation of appendix K, "Other Illegal Limitations on Credit Checklist."

Using other prohibited bases may be useful and appropriate if a bank does not have any products with at least five denials or at least five approvals from one prohibited basis group and at least 20 control group approvals. In other words, there are not enough denials and approvals for a comparative file review of either approve/deny decisions or rates/terms/conditions.

One alternative to consider is performing a comparative file review; comparing individual male to individual female applicants or to compare married joint applicants to unmarried joint applicants using the procedures in this booklet. However, if these analyses have been done in a recent fair lending examination with no problems discovered, contact the supervisory office and, if appropriate, the Compliance Policy Division to discuss whether other types of comparisons might be worthwhile.

If no worthwhile comparisons to review exist, a second alternative to consider is a review of the bank's loan policies. Select a sample based on the level of fair lending risk of at least 10 diverse applications (different products, underwriters, branches, etc.) and complete the "Other illegal Limitations on Credit Checklist" for each of the applications. Regulation B citations on the checklist are considered substantive violations for which the OCC may seek relief for persons whose credit rights were impaired.

Most of these consumer rights are not stated explicitly in terms of a prohibited basis (for example, the prohibition against discounting or excluding protected income, 12 CFR 202.6(b)(5)). Most do not require interpretation of the comparative treatment of applicants. Usually, analysis involves only whether the bank treated applicants as explicitly required by Regulation B. Obtain an explanation from the bank staff responsible for any transactions that appear to involve a violation on the checklist and evaluate each bank explanation and verify any facts that the bank cites.

A third alternative approach is for situations where obstacles exist because underwriting guidelines are unclear and/or file documentation is poor. Treat such a situation as a high-risk one for which a comparative file review should be attempted. If loan files lack data on applicants' qualifications or if the bank's standards are unclear:

1. Ask what specific factors formed the basis for the denial reasons cited on adverse action notices.

2. Using specific approved applicants, ask how the bank determined that they differed from denied applicants.

3. Use informal file comments (if any) that characterize qualifications as good, adequate, weak, etc., as points of reference.

4. Track whether credit decision makers evaluated the factor(s) identified in steps 1-3 consistently for the control and prohibited basis groups.

5. If an apparent violation is found using this alternative analysis, follow the steps delineated in this booklet for resolving potential fair lending violations (i.e., beginning with obtaining an explanation from the bank).

Appendix N: Policy Statement on Enforcement of the Equal Credit Opportunity and Fair Housing Acts

The OCC believes it appropriate to remind national banks and theirsubsidiaries of their responsibilites under these laws and that the OCC will vigorously enforce them. National banks and their subsidiaries must institute procedures to assure that all violations of the acts, including those not cited in this policy statement, will not occur. In addition, the OCC has judged failure to comply with certain specific provisions of the acts to be particularly serious and potentially warranting retrospective action to correct the condition resulting from the violations.

Enforcement Policy Statement on the Equal Credit Opportunity Act and the Fair Housing Act

This enforcement policy statement ensures that the rights of credit applicants are protected by requiring national banks to take corrective action for certain, more serious past violations of the Equal Credit Opportunity and Fair Housing acts and to be in compliance in the future. In an effort to achieve that objective, the OCC encourages voluntary correction and compliance with the acts. Whenever violations addressed by this policy statement are discovered, a national bank will be required to take action to ensure such violations will not recur and to correct the effects of those violations discovered.

The OCC generally will require national banks to take action to correct conditions resulting from violations occurring within 24 months previous to the OCC's discovery of the violations. An exception is violations concerning adverse action notices for which corrective action will be required for violations occurring within six months prior to discovery.

The OCC considers violations in the following areas serious, and will usually be subject to retrospective corrective action:

- Discouraging applicants on a prohibited basis in violation of the Fair Housing Act or sections 202.4(b) of Regulation B.
- Using credit criteria in a discriminatory manner in evaluating applications in violation of the Fair Housing Act or sections 202.4 through 202.7 of Regulation B.
- Imposing different terms on a prohibited basis in violation of the Fair

Housing Act or sections 202.4 or 202.6(b) of Regulation B.

- Requiring cosigners, guarantors, or the like on a prohibited basis in violation of section 202.7(d) of Regulation B.
- Failing to furnish separate credit histories as required by section 202.10 of Regulation B.
- Failing to provide an adequate notice of adverse action under section 202.9 of Regulation B.

This policy statement does not:

- Preclude the OCC from using any administrative authority it possesses to enforce these laws.
- Limit the OCC's discretion to take other action to correct conditions resulting from violations of these laws.
- Preclude the OCC from referring cases to the United States Attorney General.
- Foreclose a credit applicant's right to bring a civil action under the Equal Credit Opportunity Act or Fair Housing Act or to file a complaint with the Department of Justice or the Department of Housing and Urban Development for violations of housing laws.
- Supersede or substitute for any regulations or enforcement policies issued by the OCC or the Department of Housing and Urban Development under the Fair Housing Act.

Appendix O: Policy Statement on Discrimination in Lending (April 15, 1994)

The Department of Housing and Urban Development ("HUD"), the Department of Justice ("DOJ"), the Office of the Comptroller of the Currency ("OCC"), the Office of Thrift Supervision ("OTS"), the Board of Governors of the Federal Reserve System (the "Board"), the Federal Deposit Insurance Corporation ("FDIC"), the Federal Housing Finance Board ("FHFB"), the Federal Trade Commission ("FTC"), the National Credit Union Administration ("NCUA"), and the Office of Federal Housing Enterprise Oversight ("OFHEO") (collectively, "the Agencies") are concerned that some prospective home buyers and other borrowers may be experiencing discriminatory treatment in their efforts to obtain loans. The 1992 Federal Reserve Bank of Boston study on lending discrimination, Congressional hearings, and agency investigations have indicated that race is a factor in some lending decisions. Discrimination in lending on the basis of race or other prohibited factors is destructive, morally repugnant, and against the law. It prevents those who are discriminated against from enjoying the benefits of access to credit. The Agencies will not tolerate lending discrimination in any form. Further, fair lending is not inconsistent with safe and sound operations. Lenders must continue to ensure that their lending practices are consistent with safe and sound operating policies.

This policy statement applies to all lenders, including mortgage brokers, issuers of credit cards, and any other person who extends credit of any type. The policy statement is being issued for several reasons, including:

- To provide guidance about what the agencies consider in determining if lending discrimination exists; and
- To provide a foundation for future interpretations and rulemakings by the Agencies.

A number of federal statutes seek to promote fair lending. For example, the Home Mortgage Disclosure Act ("HMDA"), 12 U.SC. 2801 et seq., seeks to prevent lending discrimination and redlining by requiring public disclosure of certain information about mortgage loan applications. The Community Reinvestment Act ("CRA"), 12 U.S.C. 2901 et seq., seeks affirmatively to encourage institutions to help to meet the credit needs of the entire community served by each institution covered by the statute, and CRA ratings take into account lending discrimination by those institutions. The Americans with Disabilities Act, 42 U.S.C. 12101 et seq., prohibits discrimination against persons with disabilities in the provision of goods and services, including credit services. This policy statement, however, is based upon and addresses only the Equal Credit Opportunity Act ("ECOA"), 15 U.S.C. 1691 et seq., and the Fair Housing Act ("FH Act"), 42 U.S.C. 3601 et seq, the two statutes that specifically prohibit discrimination in lending.

This policy statement has been approved and adopted by the signatory Agencies listed above as a statement of the Agencies' general position on the ECOA and the FH Act for purposes of administrative enforcement of those statutes. It is intended to be consistent with those statutes and their implementing regulations and to provide guidance to lenders seeking to comply with them. It does not create or confer any substantive or procedural rights on third parties which could be enforceable in any administrative or civil proceeding.

This policy statement will discuss what constitutes lending discrimination under these statutes and answer questions about how the Agencies will respond to lending discrimination and what steps lenders might take to prevent discriminatory lending practices.

A. Lending Discrimination Statutes and Regulations

(1) The ECOA prohibits discrimination in any aspect of a credit transaction. The ECOA is not limited to consumer loans. It applies to any extension of credit, including extensions of credit to small businesses, corporations, partnerships, and trusts. The ECOA prohibits discrimination based on:

- Race or color;
- Religion;
- National origin;
- Sex;
- Marital status;
- Age (provided the applicant has the capacity to contract);
- The applicant's receipt of income derived from any public assistance program; and
- The applicant's exercise, in good faith, of any right under the Consumer Credit Protection Act.

The Federal Reserve Board's Regulation B, found at 12 CFR part 202, implements the ECOA. Regulation B describes lending acts and practices that are specifically prohibited, permitted, or required. Official interpretations of the regulation are found in Supplement I to 12 CFR part 202.

(2) The FH Act prohibits discrimination in all aspects of residential real- estate -related transactions, including, but not limited to:

- Making loans to buy, build, repair, or improve a dwelling;
- Purchasing real estate loans;
- Selling, brokering, or appraising residential real estate; and
- Selling or renting a dwelling.

The FH Act prohibits discrimination based on:

- Race or color;
- National origin;
- Religion;
- Sex;
- Familial status (defined as children under the age of 18 living with a parent or legal custodian, pregnant women, and people securing custody of children under 18); and
- Handicap.

HUD's regulations implementing the FH Act are found at 24 CFR Part 100.

Because both the FH Act and the ECOA apply to mortgage lending, lenders may not discriminate in mortgage lending based on any of the prohibited factors in either list.

Liability under these two statutes for discrimination on a prohibited basis is civil, not criminal. However, there is criminal liability under the FH Act for various forms of interference with efforts to enforce the FH Act, such as altering or withholding evidence or forcefully intimidating persons seeking to exercise their rights under the FH Act.

What is prohibited.. Under the ECOA, it is unlawful for a lender to discriminate on a prohibited basis in any aspect of a credit transaction and, under both the ECOA and the FH Act, it is unlawful for a lender to discriminate on a prohibited basis in a residential real estate related transaction. Under one or both of these laws, a lender may not, because of a prohibited factor:

- Fail to provide information or services or provide different information or services regarding any aspect of the lending process, including credit availability, application procedures, or lending standards;
- Discourage or selectively encourage applicants with respect to inquiries about or applications for credit;
- Refuse to extend credit or use different standards in determining whether to extend credit;
- Vary the terms of credit offered, including the amount, interest rate, duration, or type of loan;
- Use different standards to evaluate collateral;
- Treat a borrower differently in servicing a loan or invoking default remedies; or
- Use different standards for pooling or packaging a loan in the secondary market.

A lender may not express, orally or in writing, a preference based on prohibited factors or indicate that it will treat applicants differently on a prohibited basis.

A lender may not discriminate on a prohibited basis because of the characteristics of:

- A person associated with a credit applicant (for example, a co-applicant, spouse, business partner, or live-in aide); or
- The present or prospective occupants of the area where property to be financed is located.

Finally, the FH Act requires lenders to make reasonable accommodations for a person with disabilities when such accommodations are necessary to afford the person an equal opportunity to apply for credit.

B. Types of Lending Discrimination

The courts have recognized three methods of proof of lending discrimination under the ECOA and the FH Act:

- "Overt evidence of discrimination," when a lender blatantly discriminates on a prohibited basis;

- Evidence of "disparate treatment," when a lender treats applicants differently based on one of the prohibited factors; and
- Evidence of "disparate impact," when a lender applies a practice uniformly to all applicants but the practice has a discriminatory effect on a prohibited basis and is not justified by business necessity.

Overt Evidence of Discrimination.

There is overt evidence of discrimination when a lender openly discriminates on a prohibited basis.

Example: A lender offered a credit card with a limit of up to $750 for applicants aged 21-30 and $1500 for applicants over 30. This policy violated the ECOA's prohibition on discrimination based on age.

There is overt evidence of discrimination even when a lender expresses--but does not act on--a discriminatory preference:

Example: A lending officer told a customer, "We do not like to make home mortgages to Native Americans, but the law says we cannot discriminate and we have to comply with the law." This statement violated the FH Act's prohibition on statements expressing a discriminatory preference.

Evidence of Disparate Treatment.

Disparate treatment occurs when a lender treats a credit applicant differently based on one of the prohibited bases. Disparate treatment ranges from overt discrimination to more subtle disparities in treatment. It does not require any showing that the treatment was motivated by prejudice or a conscious intention to discriminate against a person beyond the difference in treatment itself. It is considered by courts to be intentional discrimination because no credible, nondiscriminatory reason explains the difference in treatment on a prohibited basis.

Example: Two minority loan applicants were told that it would take several hours and require the payment of an application fee to determine whether they would qualify for a home mortgage loan. In contrast, a loan officer took financial information immediately from nonminority applicants and determined whether they qualified in minutes, without a fee being paid. The lender's differential treatment violated both the ECOA and the FH Act.

Redlining refers to the illegal practice of refusing to make residential loans or imposing more onerous terms on any loans made because of the predominant race, national origin, etc., of the residents of the neighborhood in which the property is located. Redlining violates both the FH Act and the ECOA.

Disparate treatment may more likely occur in the treatment of applicants who are neither clearly well-qualified nor clearly unqualified. Discrimination may more readily affect applicants in this middle group for two reasons. First, because the applications are all "close cases," there is more room and need for lender discretion. Second, whether or not an applicant qualifies may depend on the level of assistance the lender provides the applicant in preparing an application. The lender may, for example, propose solutions to problems on an application, identify compensating factors, and provide encouragement to the applicant. Lenders are under no obligation to provide such assistance, but to the extent that they do, the assistance must be provided in a nondiscriminatory way.

Example: A nonminority couple applied for an automobile loan. The lender found adverse information in the couple's credit report. The lender discussed the credit report with them and determined that the adverse information, a judgment against the couple, was incorrect since the judgment had been vacated. The nonminority couple was granted their loan. A minority couple applied for a similar loan with the same lender. Upon discovering adverse information in the minority couple's credit report, the lender denied the loan application on the basis of the adverse information without giving the couple an opportunity to discuss the report.

Example: Two minority borrowers inquired with a lender about mortgage loans. They were given applications for fixed-rate loans only and were not offered assistance in completing the loan applications. They completed the applications on their own and ultimately failed to qualify. Two similarly situated nonminority borrowers made an identical inquiry about mortgage loans to the same lender. They were given information about both adjustable-rate and fixed-rate mortgages and were given assistance in preparing applications that the lender could accept.

Both of these are examples of disparate treatment of similarly situated applicants, apparently based on a prohibited factor, in the amount of assistance and information the lender provided. The lender might also generally exercise its discretion to disfavor some individuals or favor others in a manner that results in a pattern or practice of disparate treatment that cannot be explained on grounds other than a prohibited basis.

If a lender has apparently treated similar applicants differently on the basis of a prohibited factor, it must provide an explanation for the difference in treatment. If the lender is unable to provide a credible and legitimate nondiscriminatory explanation, the agency may infer that the lender discriminated.

If an agency determines that a lender's explanation for treating some applicants differently is a pretext for discrimination, the agency may find that the lender discriminated, notwithstanding the lender's explanation.

Example: A lender rejected a loan application made by a female applicant with flaws in her credit report but accepted applications by male applicants with similar flaws. The lender offered the explanation that the rejected application had been processed by a new loan officer who was unfamiliar with the bank's policy to work with applicants to correct credit report problems. However, an investigation revealed that the same loan officer who processed the rejected application had accepted applications from males with similar credit problems after working with them to provide satisfactory explanations.

When a lender's treatment of two applicants is compared, even when there is an apparently valid explanation for a particular difference in treatment, further investigation may establish disparate treatment on a prohibited basis. For example, seemingly valid explanations for denying loans to minority applicants may have been applied consistently to minority applicants and inconsistently to nonminority applicants; or "offsetting" or "compensatory" factors cited as the reason for approving nonminority applicants may involve information that the lender usually failed to consider for minority applicants but usually considered for nonminority applicants.

A pattern or practice of disparate treatment on a prohibited basis may also be established through a valid statistical analysis of detailed loan file information, provided that the analysis controls for possible legitimate explanations for differences in treatment. Where a lender's underwriting decisions are the subject of a statistical analysis, detailed information must be collected from individual loan files about the applicants' qualifications for credit. Data reported by lenders under the HMDA do not, standing alone, provide sufficient information for such an analysis because they omit important variables, such as credit histories and debt ratios. HMDA data are useful, though, for identifying lenders whose practices may warrant investigation for compliance with fair lending laws. HMDA data may also be relevant, in conjunction with other evidence, to the determination whether a lender has discriminated.

Evidence of Disparate Impact

When a lender applies a policy or practice equally to credit applicants, but the policy or practice has a disproportionate adverse impact on applicants from a group protected against discrimination, the policy or practice is described as having a "disparate impact." Policies and practices that are neutral on their face and that are applied equally may still, on a prohibited basis, disproportionately and adversely affect a person's access to credit.

Although the precise contours of the law on disparate impact as it applies to lending discrimination are under development, it has been clearly established that proof of lending discrimination using a disparate impact analysis encompasses several steps. The single fact that a policy or practice creates a disparity on a prohibited basis is not alone proof of a violation. Where the policy or practice is justified by "business necessity" and there is no less discriminatory alternative, a violation of the FH Act or the ECOA will not exist.

The existence of a disparate impact may be established through review of how a particular practice, policy or standard operates with respect to those who are affected by it. The existence of disparate impact is not established by a mere assertion or general perception that a policy or practice disproportionately excludes or injures people on a prohibited basis. The existence of a disparate impact must be established by facts. Frequently this is done through a quantitative or statistical analysis. Sometimes the operation of the practice is reviewed by analyzing its effect on an applicant pool; sometimes it consists of an analysis of the practice's effect on possible applicants, or on the population in general. Not every member of the group must be adversely affected for the practice to have a disparate impact. Evidence of discriminatory intent is not necessary to establish that a policy or practice adopted or implemented by a lender that has a disparate impact is in violation of the FH Act or ECOA.

Identifying the existence of a disparate impact is only the first step in proving lending discrimination under this method of proof. When an Agency finds that a lender's policy or practice has a disparate impact, the next step is to seek to determine whether the policy or practice is justified by "business necessity." The justification must be manifest and may not be hypothetical or speculative. Factors that may be relevant to the justification could include cost and profitability.

Even if a policy or practice that has a disparate impact on a prohibited basis can be justified by business necessity, it still may be found to be discriminatory if an alternative policy or practice could serve the same purpose with less discriminatory effect.

Example: A lender's policy is not to extend loans for single family residences for less than $60,000.00. This policy has been in effect for ten years. This minimum loan amount policy is shown to disproportionately exclude potential minority applicants from consideration because of their income levels or the value of the houses in the areas in which they live. The lender will be required to justify the "business necessity" for the policy.

Example: In the past, lenders primarily considered net income in making underwriting decisions. In recent years, the trend has been to consider gross income. A lender decided to switch its practices to consider gross income rather than net income. However, in calculating gross income, the lender did not distinguish between taxable and nontaxable income even though nontaxable income is of more value than the equivalent amount of taxable income. The lender's policy may have a disparate impact on individuals with disabilities and the elderly, both of whom are more likely than the general applicant pool to receive substantial nontaxable income. The lender's policy is likely to be proven discriminatory. First, the lender is unlikely to be able to show that the policy is compelled by business necessity. Second, even if the lender could show business necessity, the lender could achieve the same purpose with less discriminatory effect by "grossing up" nontaxable income (i.e., making it equivalent to gross taxable income by using formulas related to the applicant's tax bracket).

Lenders will not have to justify every requirement and practice every time that they face a compliance examination. The Agencies recognize the relevance to credit decisions of factors related to the adequacy of the borrower's income to carry the loan, the likely continuation of that income, the adequacy of the collateral to secure the loan, the borrower's past performance in paying obligations, the availability of funds to close, and the existence of adequate reserves. While lenders should think critically about whether widespread, familiar requirements and practices have an

---

unjustifiable disparate impact, they should look especially carefully at requirements that are more stringent than customary. Lenders should also stay informed of developments in underwriting and portfolio performance evaluation so that they are well positioned to consider all options by which their business objectives can be achieved.

C. Answers to Questions Often Asked by Financial Institutions and the Public

Lending institutions and others often ask the Agencies questions about various aspects of lending discrimination. The Agencies have compiled this list of common questions, with answers, in order to provide further guidance.

Q1: Are disparities in application, approval, or denial rates revealed by HMDA data sufficient to establish lending discrimination?

A: HMDA data alone do not prove lending discrimination. The data do not contain enough information on major credit-related factors, such as employment and credit histories, to prove discrimination. Despite these limitations, the data can provide "red flags" that there may be problems at particular institutions. Therefore, regulatory and enforcement agencies may use HMDA data, along with other factors, to identify institutions whose lending practices warrant more scrutiny. Furthermore, HMDA data can be relevant, in conjunction with other data and information, to the determination whether a lender has discriminated.

Q2: Does a lending institution that submits inaccurate HMDA data violate lending discrimination laws?

A: An inaccurate HMDA data submission constitutes a violation of the HMDA, the Federal Reserve Board's Regulation C, and other applicable laws, and may subject the lending institution to an enforcement action, which could include civil money penalties, and, if the lender is a HUD-approved mortgagee, the sanctions of the HUD Mortgagee Review Board. An inaccurate HMDA data submission, however, is not in itself a violation of the ECOA or the FH Act. However, a person who intentionally submits incorrect or incomplete HMDA data in order to cover up a violation of the FH Act may be subject, under the FH Act and federal criminal statutes, to a fine or prison term or both. In addition, a failure to ensure accurate HMDA data may be considered as a relevant fact during a FH Act investigation or an examination of the institution's lending activities.

Q3: Does a second review program only for loan applicants who are members of a protected class violate laws prohibiting discrimination in lending?

A: Such programs are permissible if they do no more than ensure that lending standards are applied fairly and uniformly to all applicants. For example, it is permissible to review the proposed denial of applicants who are members of a protected class by comparing their applications to the approved applications of similarly qualified individuals who are not members of a protected class to determine if the applications were evaluated consistently. It is impermissible, however, to review the applications of members of a protected class in order to apply standards to those applications different from the standards used to evaluate other applications for the same credit program or to apply the same standards in a different manner, unless such actions are otherwise permitted by law, as described in Question 4.

Other types of second review programs are also permissible. For example, lenders could review the proposed denial of all applicants within a certain income range. Lenders also could review a sampling of all applications proposed for denial, or even review all such applications.

Q4: May a lender apply different lending standards to applicants who are members of a protected class in order to increase lending to that sector of its community?

A: Generally, a lender that applies different lending standards or offers different levels of assistance on a prohibited basis, regardless of its motivation, would be violating both the FH Act and the ECOA. There are exceptions to the general rule; thus, applying different lending standards or offering different levels of assistance to applicants who are members of a protected class is permissible in some circumstances. For example, the FH Act requires lenders to provide reasonable accommodation to people with disabilities. In addition, providing different treatment to applicants to address past discrimination would be permissible if done in response to a court order or otherwise in accord with applicable legal precedent. However, the law in this area is complex and developing. Before implementing programs of this sort, a lender should seek legal advice.

Of course, affirmative advertising and marketing efforts that do not involve application of different lending standards are permissible under both the ECOA and the FH Act. For example, special outreach to a minority community would be permissible.

Q5: Should a lender engage in self-testing?

A: Principles of sound lending dictate that adequate policies and procedures be in place to ensure safe and sound lending practices and compliance with applicable laws and regulations, and that a lender adopt appropriate audit and control systems to determine whether the institution's policies and procedures are functioning adequately. This is as true in the area of fair lending as in other operations. Lenders should employ reliable measures for auditing fair lending compliance. A well-designed and implemented program of self-testing could be a valuable part of this process. Lenders should be aware, however, that data documenting lending discrimination discovered in a self-test generally will not be shielded from disclosure.

Corrective actions should always be taken by any lender that discovers discrimination. Self-testing and corrective actions do not expunge or extinguish legal liability for the violations of law, insulate a lender from private suits, or eliminate the primary regulatory agency's obligation to make the referrals required by law. However, they will be considered as a substantial mitigating factor by the primary regulatory agencies when contemplating possible enforcement actions. In addition, HUD and DOJ will consider as a substantial mitigating factor an institution's self-identification and self-correction when determining whether they will seek additional penalties or other relief under the FH Act and the ECOA. The Agencies strongly encourage self-testing and will consider further steps that might be taken to provide greater incentives for institutions to undertake self-assessment and self-correction.

Q6: What should a lender do if self-testing evidences lending discrimination?

A: If a lender discovers discriminatory practices, it should make all reasonable efforts to determine the full extent of the discrimination and its cause, e.g., determine whether the practices were grounded in defective policies, poor implementation or control of those policies, or isolated to a particular area of the lender's operations. The lender should take all appropriate corrective actions to address the discrimination, including, but not limited to:

- Identifying customers whose applications may have been inappropriately processed, offering to extend credit if they were improperly denied;

compensating them for any damages, both out-of-pocket and compensatory; and notifying them of their legal rights;

- Correcting any institutional policies or procedures that may have contributed to the discrimination;
- Identifying, and then training and/or disciplining, the employees involved;
- Considering the need for community outreach programs and/or changes in marketing strategy or loan products to better serve minority segments of the lender's market; and
- Improving audit and oversight systems in order to ensure there is no recurrence of the discrimination.

An institution is not required to report to the Agencies a lending discrimination problem it has discovered. However, a lender that reports its discovery can ensure that the corrective actions it develops are appropriate and complete and thereby minimize the damages to which it will be subject.

Q7: Will a lender be held responsible for discriminatory lending engaged in by a single loan officer where the lending institution has good policies and procedures in place, is otherwise in full compliance with all applicable laws and regulations, and neither knows nor reasonably could have known that the officer was engaged in illegal discriminatory conduct?

A: Fair lending violations can occur even in the most well-run lending institutions that have good policies in place to ensure compliance with fair lending laws and regulations. Of course, the chances that such violations will occur can be greatly reduced by backing up those policies with proper employee training and supervision and subjecting the lending process to proven systems of oversight and review. Self-testing can further reduce the likelihood that violations may occur. Notwithstanding these efforts, a single loan officer might still improperly apply policies or, worse yet, deliberately circumvent them and manage to conceal or disguise the true nature of his or her practices for a time. It may be particularly difficult to discover this type of behavior when it occurs in the pre-application process.

In any case where discriminatory lending by a lending institution is identified, the lender will be expected to identify and fairly compensate victims of discriminatory conduct just as it would be expected to compensate a customer if an employee's conduct resulted in physical injury to the customer. In addition, such a violation might constitute a "pattern or practice" that must be referred to DOJ or a violation that must be referred to HUD.

As in other cases of discriminatory behavior, where a lender takes self-initiated corrective actions, such actions will be considered as a substantial mitigating factor by the Agencies in determining the nature of any enforcement action and what penalties or other relief would be appropriate.

Q8: If a federal financial institutions regulatory agency has "reason to believe" that a lender has engaged in a pattern or practice of discrimination in violation of the ECOA, the ECOA requires the agency to refer the matter to DOJ. What constitutes a "reason to believe"?

A: A federal financial institutions regulatory agency has reason to believe that an ECOA violation has occurred when a reasonable person would conclude from an examination of all credible information available that discrimination has occurred. This determination requires weighing the available evidence and applicable law and determining whether an apparent violation has occurred. Information supporting a reason to believe finding may include loan files and other documents, credible observations by persons with direct knowledge, statistical analysis, and the financial institution's response to the preliminary examination findings.

Reason to believe is more than an unfounded suspicion. While the evidence of discrimination need not be definitive and need not include evidence of overt discrimination, it should be developed to the point that a reasonable person would conclude that a violation exists.

Q9: If a federal financial institutions regulatory agency has reason to believe that a lender has engaged in a "pattern or practice" of discrimination in violation of the ECOA, the agency will refer the matter to DOJ. What constitutes a "pattern or practice" of lending discrimination?

A: Determinations by federal financial institutions regulatory agencies regarding a pattern or practice of lending discrimination must be based on an analysis of the facts in a given case. Isolated, unrelated or accidental occurrences will not constitute a pattern or practice. However, repeated, intentional, regular, usual, deliberate, or institutionalized practices will almost always constitute a pattern or practice. The totality of the circumstances must be considered when assessing whether a pattern or practice is present. Considerations include, but are not limited to:

- Whether the conduct appears to be grounded in a written or unwritten policy or established practice that is discriminatory in purpose or effect;

- Whether there is evidence of similar conduct by a financial institution toward more than one applicant. Note, however, that this is not a mathematical process, e.g., "more than one" does not necessarily constitute a pattern or practice;
- Whether the conduct has some common source or cause within the financial institution's control;
- The relationship of the instances of conduct to one another (e.g., whether they all occurred in the same area of the financial institution's operations); and
- The relationship of the number of instances of conduct to the financial institution's total lending activity. Note, however, that, depending on the circumstances, violations that involve only a small percentage of an institution's total lending activity could constitute a pattern or practice.

Depending on the egregiousness of the facts and circumstances involved, singly or in combination, these factors could provide evidence of a pattern or practice.

Q10: How does the employment of few minorities and individuals from other protected classes in lending positions--e.g., Account Executive, Underwriter, Loan Counselor, Loan Processor, Staff Appraiser, Assistant Branch Manager and Branch Manager--affect compliance with lending discrimination laws?

A: The employment of few minorities and others in protected classes, in itself, is not a violation of the FH Act or the ECOA. However, employment of few members of protected classes in lending positions can contribute to a climate in which lending discrimination could occur by affecting the delivery of services.

Therefore, lenders might consider the following steps, as appropriate to their institutions:

- Advertising lending job openings in local minority-oriented publications;
- Notifying predominantly minority organizations of such openings;
- Seeking employment referrals from current minority employees, minority real estate boards and local historically minority colleges and other institutions that serve minority groups in the community; and
- Seeking qualified independent fee appraisers from local minority appraisal organizations.

Similar outreach steps could be considered to recruit women, persons with disabilities, and other persons protected by the FH Act and the ECOA.

Q11: What is the role of the guidelines of secondary market purchasers and private and governmental loan insurers in determining whether primary lenders practice lending discrimination?

A: Many lenders make mortgage loans only when they can be sold on the secondary market, or they may place some loans in their own portfolios and sell others on the secondary market. The principal secondary market purchasers, Federal National Mortgage Association ("Fannie Mae") and Federal Home Loan Mortgage Corporation ("Freddie Mac"), publish underwriting guidelines to inform primary lenders of the conditions under which they will buy loans. For example, ability to repay the loan is measured by suggested ratios of monthly housing expense to income (28%) and total obligations to income (36%). However, these guidelines allow considerable discretion on the part of the primary lender. In addition, the secondary market guidelines have in some cases been made more flexible, for example, with respect to factors such as stability of income (rather than stability of employment) and use of nontraditional ways of establishing good credit and ability to pay (e.g., use of past rent and utility payment records). Lenders should ensure that their loan processors and underwriters are aware of the provisions of the secondary market guidelines that provide various alternative and flexible means by which applicants may demonstrate their ability and willingness to repay their loans. Fannie Mae and Freddie Mac not infrequently purchase mortgages exceeding the suggested ratios, and their guidelines contain detailed discussions of the compensating factors that can justify higher ratios (and which must be documented by the primary lender).

A lender who rejects an application from an applicant who is a member of a protected class and who has ratios above those of the guidelines and approves an application from another applicant with similar ratios should be prepared to show that the reason for the rejection was based on factors that are applied consistently without regard to any of the prohibited factors.

These same principles apply equally to the guidelines of private and governmental loan insurers.

Q12: What criteria will be employed in taking enforcement actions or seeking remedial measures when lending discrimination is discovered?

A: Enforcement sanctions and remedial measures for lending discrimination violations vary depending on whether such sanctions are sought by the appropriate federal financial institutions regulatory agencies, DOJ, HUD or other federal agencies charged with enforcing either the ECOA or the FH Act. The following discussion sets out the criteria typically employed by the federal banking agencies (i.e., OCC, OTS, the Board and FDIC), NCUA, DOJ, HUD, OFHEO, FHFB, and FTC in determining the nature and severity of sanctions that may be used to address discriminatory lending practices. As discussed in Questions 8 and 9, above, in certain situations, the primary regulatory agencies will also refer enforcement matters to HUD or DOJ.

The federal banking agencies:

The federal banking agencies are authorized to use the full range of their enforcement authority under 12 U.S.C. 1818 to address discriminatory lending practices. This includes the authority to seek:

- Enforcement actions that may require both prospective and retrospective relief; and
- Civil money penalties ("CMPs") in varying amounts against the financial institution or any institution-affiliated party ("IAP") within the meaning of 12 U.S.C. 1813(u), depending, among other things, on the nature of the violation and the degree of culpability.

In addition to the above actions, the federal banking agencies may also take removal and prohibition actions against any IAP where the statutory requirements for such actions are met.

The federal banking agencies will make determinations as to the appropriateness of any potential enforcement action after giving full consideration to a variety of factors. In making these determinations, the banking agencies will take into account:

- The number and duration of violations identified;
- The nature of the evidence of discrimination (i.e., overt discrimination, disparate treatment or disparate impact);
- Whether the discrimination was limited to a particular office or unit of the financial institution or was more pervasive in nature;
- The presence and effectiveness of any anti-discrimination policies;
- Any history of discriminatory conduct; and

- Any corrective measures implemented or proposed by the financial institution.

The severity of the federal banking agencies' enforcement response will depend on the egregiousness of the financial institution's conduct. Voluntary identification and correction of violations disclosed through a self-testing program will be a substantial mitigating factor in considering whether to initiate an enforcement action.

In addition, the federal banking agencies may consider whether an institution has provided victims of discrimination with all the relief available to them under applicable civil rights laws.

The federal banking agencies may seek both prospective and retrospective relief for fair lending violations.

Prospective relief may include requiring the financial institution to:

- Adopt corrective policies and procedures and correct any financial institution policies or procedures that may have contributed to the discrimination;
- Train financial institution employees involved;
- Establish community outreach programs and change marketing strategy or loan products to better serve all sectors of the financial institution's service area;
- Improve internal audit controls and oversight systems in order to ensure there is no recurrence of discrimination; or
- Monitor compliance and provide periodic reports to the primary federal regulator.

Retrospective relief may include:

- Identifying customers who may have been subject to discrimination and offering to extend credit if the customers were improperly denied;
- Requiring the financial institution to make payments to injured parties:
- Restitution: This may include any out-of-pocket expenses incurred as a result of the violation to make the victim of discrimination whole, such as: fees or expenses in connection with the application; the difference between any greater fees or expenses of another loan granted elsewhere after denial by the discriminating lender; and, when loans were granted on

disparate terms, appropriate modification of those terms and refunds of any greater amounts paid.

- Other Affirmative Action As Appropriate to Correct Conditions Resulting From Discrimination: The federal banking agencies also have the authority to require a financial institution to take affirmative action to correct or remedy any conditions resulting from any violation or practice. The banking agencies will determine whether such affirmative action is appropriate in a given case and, if such action is appropriate, the type of remedy to order.

- Requiring the financial institution to pay CMPs:

The banking agencies have the authority to assess CMPs against financial institutions or individuals for violating fair lending laws or regulations. Each agency has the authority to assess CMPs of up to $5,000 per day for any violation of law, rule or regulation. Penalties of up to $25,000 per day are also permitted, but only if the violations represent a pattern of misconduct, cause more than minimal loss to the financial institution, or result in gain or benefit to the party involved. CMPs are paid to the U.S. Treasury and therefore do not compensate victims of discrimination.

National Credit Union Administration

For federal credit unions, NCUA will employ criteria comparable to those of the federal banking agencies, pursuant to its authority under 12 U.S.C. 1786.

The Department of Justice

The Department of Justice is authorized to use the full range of its enforcement authority under the FH Act and the ECOA. DOJ has authority to commence pattern or practice investigations of possible lending discrimination on its own initiative or through referrals from the federal financial institutions regulatory agencies, and to file lawsuits in federal court where there is reasonable cause to believe that such violations have occurred. DOJ is also authorized under the FH Act to bring suit based on individual complaints filed with HUD where one of the parties to the complaint elects to have the case heard in federal court.

The relief sought by DOJ in lending discrimination lawsuits may include:

- An injunction which may require both prospective and retrospective relief; and,

- In enforcement actions under the FH Act, CMPs not to exceed $50,000 per defendant for a first violation and $100,000 for any subsequent violation.

Prospective injunctive relief may include:

A permanent injunction to insure against a recurrence of the unlawful practices;
Affirmative measures to correct past discriminatory policies, procedures, or practices, so long as consistent with safety and soundness, such as:

- Expansion of the lender's service areas to include previously excluded minority neighborhoods;
- Opening branches or other credit facilities in under-served minority neighborhoods;
- Targeted sales calls on real estate agents and builders active in minority neighborhoods;
- Advertising through minority-oriented media; Self-testing;
- Employee training;
- Changes to commission structures which tend to discourage lending in minority and low-income neighborhoods;
- Changes in loan processing and underwriting procedures (including second reviews of denied applications) to ensure equal treatment without regard to prohibited factors; and
- Record keeping and reporting requirements to monitor compliance with remedial obligations.

Retrospective injunctive relief may include relief for victims of past discrimination, actual and punitive damages, and offers or adjustments of credit or other forms of loan commitments.

The Department of Housing and Urban Development

The Department of Housing and Urban Development is fully authorized to investigate complaints alleging discrimination in lending in violation of the FH Act and has the authority to initiate complaints and investigations even when an individual complaint has not been received. HUD issues determinations on whether or not reasonable cause exists to believe that the FH Act has been violated. HUD also may authorize actions for temporary and preliminary injunctions to be brought by DOJ and has authority to issue enforceable subpoenas for information related to investigations.

Following issuance of a determination of reasonable cause under the FH Act, HUD enforces the FH Act administratively unless one of the parties elects to have the case heard in federal court in a case brought by DOJ.

Relief under the FH Act that may be awarded by an administrative law judge ("ALJ") after a hearing, or by the Secretary on review of a decision by an ALJ, includes:

- Injunctive or other appropriate relief, including a variety of actions designed to correct discriminatory practices, such as changes in loan processes or procedures, modifications of loan service areas or branching actions, approval of previously denied loans to aggrieved persons, additional record-keeping and reporting on future activities or other affirmative relief;
- Actual damages suffered by persons who are aggrieved by any violation of the FH Act, including damages for mental distress and out-of-pocket losses attributable to a violation; and
- Civil penalties of up to $10,000 for each initial violation and up to $25,000 and $50,000 for successive violations within specific time frames.

HUD also is authorized to direct Fannie Mae and Freddie Mac to undertake various remedial actions, including suspension, probation, reprimand, or settlement, against lenders found to have engaged in discriminatory lending practices in violation of the FH Act or the ECOA.

The Office of Federal Housing Enterprise Oversight

The Office of Federal Housing Enterprise Oversight is authorized to use its enforcement authority under 12 U.S.C. 4631 and 4636, including cease and desist orders and CMPs for violations by Fannie Mae and Freddie Mac of the fair housing regulations promulgated by the Secretary of HUD pursuant to 12 U.S.C. Sec. 4545.

The Federal Housing Finance Board

While the Federal Housing Finance Board does not have enforcement authority under the ECOA or the FH Act, in reviewing the members of the Federal Home Loan Bank System for community support, it may restrict access to long-term System advances to any member that, within two years prior to the due date of submission of a Community Support Statement, had a final administrative or judicial ruling against it based on violations of those statutes (or any similar state or local law prohibiting discrimination in lending). System members in this situation are asked to submit to the Finance Board an explanation of steps taken to remedy the violation or prevent a recurrence. See 12 U.S.C. 1430(g); 12 CFR 936.3 (b)(5).

The Federal Trade Commission

The Federal Trade Commission enforces the requirements of the ECOA and Regulation B for all lenders subject to the ECOA, except where enforcement is specifically committed to another agency. The FTC may exercise all of its functions and powers under the Federal Trade Commission Act ("FTC Act") to enforce the ECOA, and a violation of any requirement under the ECOA is deemed to be a violation of a requirement under the FTC Act. The FTC has the power to enforce Regulation B in the same manner as if a violation of Regulation B were a violation of an FTC trade regulation rule.

This means that the FTC has the power to investigate lenders suspected of lending discrimination and to use compulsory process in doing so. The Commission, through DOJ or on its own behalf where the Justice Department declines to act, may file suit in federal court against suspected violators and seek relief including:

- Injunctions against the violative practice;
- Civil penalties of up to $10,000 for each violation; and
- Redress to affected consumers.

In addition, the Commission routinely imposes recordkeeping and reporting requirements to monitor compliance.

Q13: Will a financial institution be subjected to multiple actions by DOJ or HUD and its primary regulator if discriminatory practices are discovered?

A: In all cases where referrals to other agencies are made, the appropriate federal financial institutions regulatory agency will engage in ongoing consultations with DOJ or HUD regarding coordination of each agency's actions. The Agencies will coordinate their enforcement actions and make every effort to eliminate unnecessarily duplicative actions. Where both a federal financial institutions regulatory agency and either DOJ or HUD are contemplating taking actions under their own respective authorities, the Agencies will seek to coordinate their actions to ensure that each agency's action is consistent and complementary. The financial institutions regulatory agencies also will discuss referrals on a case-by-case basis with DOJ or HUD to determine whether multiple actions are necessary and appropriate.

References

Laws

42 USC 3601-3619	Civil Rights Act of 1968 (Fair Housing Act)
24 CFR 100-110	Fair Housing Regulation
15 USC 1691 et seq.	Equal Credit Opportunity Act
12 CFR 202	Equal Credit Opportunity Regulation (Regulation B)

OCC Issuances

Advisory Letter 96-3, "Fair Lending: Pilot Testing Program"

Advisory Letter 98-9, "Access to Financing for Minority Small Businesses"

Banking Bulletin 92-17, "Guide to Fair Mortgage Lending"

Banking Bulletin 93-30, "Joint Statement on Fair Lending Expectations"

Banking Circular 263, "National Bank Fair Lending Efforts"

OCC Bulletin 97-24, "Credit Scoring Models"